IN SEARCH OF
MYTHS & HEROES

IN SEARCH OF
MYTHS & HEROES
MICHAEL WOOD

This book is published to accompany the television series
In Search of Myths & Heroes
produced by Maya Vision and first broadcast on BBC2 in 2005
Producer: Rebecca Dobbs

First published 2005. Copyright © Michael Wood 2005
The moral right of the author has been asserted

ISBN 0 563 52187 2

Published by BBC Books, BBC Worldwide Limited,
Woodlands, 80 Wood Lane, London W12 0TT

Commissioning editor: Sally Potter Project editor: Martin Redfern
Designer: Linda Blakemore Picture researcher: Sarah Hopper
Cartographer: Olive Pearson Production controller: Alix McCulloch

Set in Garamond Simoncini and Futura by BBC Worldwide Limited
Colour origination and printing by Butler & Tanner Ltd, Frome, England

INTRODUCTION

OVER THE YEARS MY JOB AS A FILM-MAKER, pursuing stories in history, has taken me on many thrilling journeys: searching for the tale of Troy; tracking Alexander the Great into the heart of Asia; following the epic journeys of the Conquistadors in Amazonia, Peru and Mexico. Often, in the wilds of the Hindu Kush, say, or camped among pilgrims under the sacred peaks of the Andes, I have sat by the campfire to hear legendary tales of real historical figures and events: how, for example, Alexander was borne up to heaven on a magic chariot drawn by griffons; or how he plumbed the depths of the ocean in a diving bell. Among the nomads of Central Asia I was told about his two horns, concealed by his long wavy hair (so only his barber knew his dark secret!). In Uzbekistan I heard the story of Alexander as a mirror of justice and a philosopher prince who was given earthly power by Allah; on the other hand the Zoroastrians in Iran spoke of his wicked deeds, and how he was for ever cursed for burning their holy book.

Listening to such tales it often seemed to me that among the ordinary people the legend had become more important than the history. The continued retelling of the story in the folk tradition had produced its own narrative, accumulating fabulous detail over many centuries; ending up far more wonderful than mere historical fact, but still in some mysterious way reflecting a kind of crystallized essence of the original story. In the countries of the Andes where the Inca language – Quechua – is still spoken, poems and folk plays have long been recited about Atahualpa, the Inca king who foolishly allowed himself to be trapped and bamboozled by the Spanish; today, however, he is remembered by Inca poets as a tragic, Hamlet-like figure, a noble symbol of resistance. Such experiences set me thinking about myths and hero stories in general, about the way they are passed on over time, and also about their relation to so-called 'real' history. This book, and the films that go with it, are the result of those musings.

The book tells the story of four journeys in pursuit of famous myths and heroes – and one heroine. The tales come from four of the world's richest myth-making traditions: Indian, Greek, Jewish and Celtic. These stories – a paradise myth, a tale of the hero's quest, a myth of a woman of power, and a chivalric romance about a golden age – are largely the invention of many generations of story-tellers; but my search for them took me on real journeys to real places, to the living descendants of the ancient cultures that produced the stories. In such places I hoped to touch on a deeper past at a time when the horizons of our world are perceptibly narrowing, with the erasing of old cultures and their ways of doing and thinking.

So these are four journeys in search of ancient myth and ancient history, and their living links with our present. They take us to some of the most fascinating parts of the world, from Tibet to the Horn of Africa, Arabia, Greece, the Caucasus and the far west of Ireland. They are not about narrative history but about the layers of story-telling over time. But such things are no less fascinating, particularly because of the way history, from the moment it is enacted, enters a process of myth-making, and often shades into fairy-tale. So I hope these tales add up to more than the sum of their parts. They are not just inquiries into the bare bones of historical narrative; they are also about our connections with a past that, in our age of globalization, is receding from us at an ever faster rate. Looking at such stories shows the way human beings over the millennia have created myths, played with them, and adapted them to suit their needs. It shows too how myths can become historical 'facts', and how historical people and events can often find their way into myths. I hope these journeys in search of myths and heroes prove as fascinating to you when reading about them as they were to me when making them, and that they show it is still possible, even in the twenty-first century, to travel into another time.

THE SEARCH
FOR SHANGRI-LA

To Conway, seeing it at first, it might have been a vision fluttering out of that solitary rhythm in which lack of oxygen had encompassed all his faculties. It was indeed a strange and half incredible sight. A group of coloured pavilions clung to the mountainside with the chance delicacy of flower petals impaled upon a crag. It was superb and exquisite. Beyond that, in a dazzling pyramid, soared the snow slopes of Karakal. The floor of the valley, hazily distant, welcomed the eye with greenness; sheltered from the winds, it looked to Conway a delightfully favoured place, though if it were inhabited its community must be completely isolated by the lofty and sheerly unscalable ranges on the further side. Conway experienced, as he gazed, a slight tightening of apprehension. But the feeling was only momentary, and soon merged in the deeper sensation, half mystical, half visual, of having reached at last some place that was an end, a finality.

JAMES HILTON *Lost Horizon* 1933

FULL-MOON NIGHT IN KATHMANDU, and the temples are crowded. By the Bagmati river the funeral pyres crackle and glow, as the rajahs of the dead stoke the cremation fires, cracking the skulls sharply with their sticks to release the spirits, and watching the sparks swirl above the darkening forest till they disappear from sight. A troop of monkeys, plump and sleek, lopes across the bridge, a hirsute street gang eyeing up unwary tourists. Beyond the trees, around the great stupa at Bodnath with its huge painted eyes, red-cloaked monks circle the stands of puja lamps, and tourists crowd the rooftop cafés sipping hot chocolate as the last light falls from the rim of the world, and a sudden chill descends.

Previous pages: The borderland of Nepal and Tibet, viewed from our plane as we approached the town of Simikot.
Opposite: A traditional map of the mythical land of Shambala, surrounded by its ring of peaks with the palace at the centre.
Above: Monks lighting prayer lamps on full-moon night at Bodnath stupa, Kathmandu.

To the traveller, Kathmandu is more than a physical crossing place between the plains of India, the Himalayas and the high Tibetan plateau; it is the meeting place between the Hindu religion, with all its many-armed wonders, and the austere metaphysical bent of the Tibetan imagination. In the great yard around the stupa, thousands take the evening air, while tinkling bells and deep-voiced Buddhist chants play around them in waves of sound. Despite the guerrilla war in the countryside, the lamplit shops around the courtyard are doing a roaring trade in Tibetan bric-à-brac: bronzes, flags, wood and brightly painted cloth hangings. There are devotional paintings from tantric Buddhism, Green and White Tara, and the Buddha of Compassion: benevolent deities and angry spirits, images of bliss and terror, lust and peace. In the café I stir the residue of chocolate, and in my mind's eye stare over the streamers and prayer flags and up over the rooftops, away from the balcony where we are sitting. High above the crowded valley, though we cannot see them through the darkening pall that hangs permanently over the city these days, the Himalayan snow peaks are gleaming in the moonlight.

Later in the old town, in the aptly named Pilgrims Bookstore, I rummage among stacks of old travellers' tales – stories told by soul guides, pilgrims, mountain climbers, touchers of the void, who have all come here seeking enlightenment and adventure. Breathing the mingled scent of incense and DDT, I begin to feel the light-headedness, the elation, that comes on the eve of a great adventure. Tomorrow we go by light plane to western Nepal on the first stage of a journey which we hope will lead to the remotest part of Tibet. Out there is the most sacred place on earth for Hindus and Buddhists: the holy mountain, Kailash, around which legends have gathered for centuries, perhaps millennia. Our journey, we hope, will take us even further across the high plateau of Tibet, to the still inaccessible ruins of the mysterious medieval Buddhist kingdom of Guge, the lost realm of the west which may be the model behind one of the most ancient Tibetan myths, and ultimately, of the famous legend of the lost valley of Shangri-La.

According to the Tibetan lamas there are two kinds of journey, for all journeys are both inner and outer, physical journeys and journeys of the mind. There are outward travels to specific pilgrimage places, and inward ones, through meditation and contemplation, to the sacred world of tantra and self-realization. The stages of a sacred journey, then, are linked to the stages of enlightenment. In their eyes a journey is worth little if it is merely to get from A to B.

'Are there still places like Shangri-La in Tibet?' I had asked a Tibetan monk back in London.

'Oh yes,' he replied. 'Go there and you will discover them.'

Above: Hindu holy man in Kathmandu holding the trident of Shiva. Such men (and women) still walk the sacred paths into the high Himalaya.
Overleaf: A Hindu temple in the Kathmandu valley.

THE MYTH OF AN EARTHLY PARADISE

Among the most enduring myths is the tale of an earthly paradise. From Sumerian epic to the Islands of the Blest in Celtic literature, this has been a recurring theme in the mythologies of the world. In our age of globalization and environmental crisis, encoded memories of humanity which have been shaped over thousands, and sometimes tens of thousands, of years have been rubbed away in a few generations. Not surprisingly, then, modern people have also been drawn to the dream of a lost paradise where the ravages of time and history have been held back; where human beings live in harmony with nature; and where the wisdom of the planet is saved for future generations: in other words, a Shangri-La.

Shangri-La itself, though, is a modern myth, invented by James Hilton in his 1933 novel *Lost Horizon*. Set in the troubled years before the Second World War, the book tells of a community in a lost valley in Tibet, a lamasery, or monastery, cut off from the world and time, where the wisdom of the human race is gathered against the threat of imminent catastrophe. The tale struck a chord: even the presidential retreat at Camp David was called Shangri-La. When Hilton's novel was turned into a Hollywood movie by Frank Capra, it was a great hit of the time, although the film's pacifist theme was edited out for Second World War audiences. Now the name is part of the language, used everywhere from Nepali airlines and Chinese hotels to holiday cottages in Florida and Torquay. A not quite unattainable dream.

Hilton's novel was a tale for its times. In the increasingly pessimistic 1930s the story of a kind of earthly paradise had an irresistible appeal at a time when Western civilization seemed bent on a path to self-destruction; when, as Carl Jung put it, 'the smell of burning was in the air'. And Tibet in the 1930s was still a land of mystery, one of the last unmapped places; a forbidden country on which the veil had lifted only slightly after a British expedition led by Colonel Francis Younghusband in 1904. Now, of course, the choice of Tibet as the location of the tale is all the more poignant given what has happened there since, with the Chinese invasion of 1959 and the deliberate devastation of its ancient culture in the Cultural Revolution of the mid-1960s.

In the novel a group of Westerners is rescued by plane from war and chaos in

Opposite: Poster for the 1937 film of James Hilton's novel *Lost Horizon*, directed by Frank Capra. In choosing the setting, Hilton was strongly influenced by early accounts of western Tibet.

Central Asia, only to crash-land in a remote valley on the roof of the world. The location of the fictional lost valley is never precisely pinpointed, but on its last fateful flight the plane appears to be heading northeast from Afghanistan across the Karakorum, and Hilton clearly imagined it somewhere in the then unexplored far west of Tibet. Headed by a 200-year-old Capuchin lama, the monastery is a repository of the cultural treasures of the planet, its inhabitants opposed to all violence and materialism. Hilton tells us that the monastery stood in the shadow of a magnificent white mountain, 'the loveliest mountain on earth … an almost perfect cone of snow, a dazzling pyramid so radiant, so serenely poised that it scarcely seemed to be real'. But where did the story come from? Did Hilton have an actual place in mind? Was there indeed a real Shangri-La? And why has the myth of an earthly paradise had such a hold on the human imagination? Those were the questions I carried with me as I began my quest.

THE DISCOVERY OF TIBET

Like all great stories the tale didn't come out of the air. The British invasion in 1904 had increased Western knowledge of Tibet. After the horrors of the First World War, the idea of a surviving ancient civilization that was founded on the peaceful principles of Buddhism began to exert a powerful fascination, which was compounded by the speculations of New Age mystics and theosophists such as Annie Besant and the Russian Nicholas Roerich. Then extraordinary photographs of the landscape and temples of western Tibet were published for the first time by the Italian explorer Tucci in 1932, at the very moment when Hilton was writing. These things were in the air. But in fact the tale of a lost kingdom in that region had first come to Western attention nearly four centuries before. And like many a tale of lost treasure it starts with a mysterious map.

A hundred years ago in Calcutta a remarkable manuscript was discovered, which contained the autobiography of a Western missionary in the court of the Moghul emperor Akbar in the 1580s. This was a glorious time in which India was at the centre of the civilized world. But it was also the moment when the axis of history was shifting, its centre of gravity moving towards the Western seaboard and away from the Asiatic heartland of the traditional civilizations, then in their final flowering – Ming, Moghuls, Savafids, Ottomans: high civilizations about to be eclipsed for ever by the impact of modernity as construed and constructed by Europeans.

In the late sixteenth century, when Akbar came to the throne, the conquest of the New World was well under way, and in the Christian West learned men debated the nature of civilization, even asking whether the non-European peoples of the Americas had souls at all. In India at this time Akbar gathered scholars of many countries around him, hoping to find the common basis of all religions, in order to remove the sources of religious conflict for the good of humankind. 'It now becomes clear,' said Akbar, 'that it cannot be right to assert the truth of one faith above any other ... In this way we may perhaps again open the door whose key has been lost.'

Although a Muslim, Akbar was fascinated by the 'eternal wisdom' of his Hindu subjects. He sent an expedition to find the source of the sacred river Ganges, and they came back with information about the Himalayan world till then known only to the ascetics and sadhus. These were men who practised their austerities in ice caves on the roof of the world, sometimes (as they still do) staying all year round in a wilderness of rock and snow, immersing themselves in the icy embrace of Mother Ganga, covered only with the ash of Shiva; men who by controlling their tapas, their inner heat, can slow their metabolism to withstand the terrible cold and deprivation.

In Akbar's audience hall these amazing stories were recounted before his international guests, who must have felt as if they were hearing tales from outer space. This was the moment when Westerners first heard accounts of what lay beyond the mountains, the very first time Tibet entered the consciousness of Europeans. 'These yogis are prone to tell the tallest tales!' wrote a Jesuit missionary present in the court, Father Monserrate, 'but according to them, beyond the Himalayas lies a great plateau where humans live.' Father Monserrate then jotted down the things he had learned from the yogis in a notebook, and he summarized them in the map found in Calcutta. On the map the area of Tibet is depicted as a great white blank, except for one place. Above the sources of the sacred rivers Ganges and Jumna is a great lake, the only place name of Tibet to be labelled: *Masarvor Lacus* – lake Manasarovar – and next to it is scribbled a tantalizing note: 'Here it is said Christians live.'

It was an extraordinary tale. But further information about Tibet came from others present in the audience hall. A Muslim merchant claimed to know more about the region, and even to have been there, perhaps on a trade route through Ladakh. The kingdom had cities, and many people – and, even better, it had a name: Shambala.

SHANGRI-LA AND SHAMBALA

Now on that name, as we shall see, there hangs quite a tale. The name first appears in a Buddhist text, which since the fourteenth century has been part of the ritual texts of Tibetan Buddhism: the *Kalachakra tantra*. In it Shambala appears as a mystical conception, a spiritual rather than a geographical goal. But curiously, although the tale is known now as a Tibetan myth, it seems that it was first recorded in AD 962 in India. The gist of the tale is of a land behind the Himalayas where the people lived in peace and harmony, faithful to the principles of Buddhism, a magic land in the shadow of a magnificent white mountain. As one commentator on the *Kalachakra tantra* put it:

> The land of Shambala lies in a valley. It is only approachable through a ring of snow peaks like the petals of a lotus … At the centre is a nine-storey crystal mountain which stands over a sacred lake, and a palace adorned with lapis, coral, gems and pearls. Shambala is a kingdom where humanity's wisdom is spared from the destructions and corruptions of time and history, ready to save the world in its hour of need.

It was, of course, a fairy-tale. Or was it? On this question much ink has been spilt. The mystical idea of Shambala first came to the West in the nineteenth century through the Hungarian explorer and mystic Cosmina de Koros; theosophists such as Annie Besant, Madame Blavatsky and Nicholas Roerich saw Shambala as the key to the secret doctrines of Tibet handed down by lamas; indeed in some circles it is still seen that way today.

Above: The Holy Family of Shiva and Parvati, the daughter of the Himalayas, on Mount Kailash. Kailash is identified as the home of the gods as far back as the early Indian epic, the *Mahabharata*.

This is how the present Dalai Lama puts it: 'Nowadays, no one knows where Shambala is. Although it is said to exist, people cannot see it, or communicate with it in an ordinary way. Some people say it is located in another world, others that it is an ideal land, a place of the imagination. Some say it was a real place which cannot now be found. Some believe there are openings into that world which may be accessed from this. Whatever the truth of that, the search for Shambala traditionally begins as an outer journey that becomes a journey of inner exploration and discovery.'

Whatever Shambala was or was not (and as we shall see, there is much more to the tale than meets the eye), the mysterious map and the tales from Akbar's court mark the beginning of the quest. For the next four centuries Western seekers – travellers, explorers and mystics – risked their lives to find this secret Tibet. The first, though, were the missionaries. This, remember, was the age when Westerners went out to the world armed with the Christian faith. From Peru and Amazonia to Goa and Japan, the Jesuits were the shock troops, the spiritual SAS, scarcely less inured to privation than the yogis by the meditative techniques of their order. It was inevitable that they should try to go to the unknown world beyond the mountains, especially with the tantalizing story that Christians lived there. Did this tale, they wondered, connect with strange medieval legends of a kingdom towards China ruled by the legendary Prester John? Or was it perhaps a hitherto unknown culture whose rituals resembled those of the Christians? Could it on the other hand be a lost Christian community, evangelized in ancient times, whose traditions had been corrupted but still preserved links with the true faith? These questions were to be answered by an intrepid young Jesuit, the first Westerner to cross the Himalayas and see the civilization of Tibet. His name was Antonio Andrade, and his now forgotten journey, one of most fascinating in history, was the journey I set out to trace, hoping it would open up new perspectives on the tales of Shambala and Shangri-La.

THE JOURNEY BEGINS

Many gurus have described the way to Shambala … but all insist that only enlightened beings, accomplished yogis steeped in spiritual discipline can possibly overcome the obstacles, physical and spiritual, which lie on the way … The seeker must have absolute faith that Shambala does indeed exist; he or she must have accumulated merit in this lifetime by good works, and must be completely detached from worldly goods and desires. Otherwise the journey will come to nothing.

By the last years of Akbar's reign there were hints that Westerners, inspired by the rumours, had attempted to get into Tibet; at least one friar had tried, but daunted by altitude and climate, lost his nerve and turned back. In 1602 Bento de Goes travelled up in a great arc from Kashmir through Central Asia to Peking, but he did not get into Tibet. Then in March 1624 Andrade came to Delhi from Agra with the Moghul court. Already fascinated by the stories about the lost world beyond the Himalayas, Andrade learned that a large party of Hindus was about to start from Delhi on a pilgrimage to a famous temple high in the mountains, about two and a half months' journey on foot. The temple was the shrine of Vishnu at Badrinath, which stood within striking distance of the passes into Tibet. Here was the opportunity he had been craving. Without waiting for permission from his superiors, Andrade decided to hitch a lift with the pilgrims. In those days caste rules forbade Hindus to rub shoulders with foreigners, and it was impossible for Westerners to travel to the sacred sites, so on the morning of his departure Andrade and his companion, who spoke Hindi, disguised themselves as Hindus, with cloak and turban, sandal paste and vermilion. Even the Delhi Christians failed to recognize them.

Andrade's account of his journey was published in 1626, but a summary in English had come out not long before Hilton wrote. In Hilton's book, when the Westerners arrive in Shangri-La they inspect the monastery's library. There on a shelf, among the great works of the literature of the world, is a copy of Andrade's *Discovery of Tibet*: a knowing wink by the author, but also perhaps another clue to where the idea for Shangri-La came from. Andrade's account would be my guide over the next dramatic weeks as I set out to retrace his footsteps from the plains of India on to the roof of the world.

The first stage of their expedition – and ours – was the well-trodden pilgrim route from Delhi to Hardwar which these days can be done in a few hours at a gentle pace by train. Hardwar is one of the holy cities of India, where the sacred river Ganges pours out of a rocky defile and enters the plains. It's a very beautiful place, where the river flows between wooded hills, cold blue and clean, rushing over a wide pebbly bed. From dawn to dusk people bathe and chant, and in the evening the priests light huge candelabra whose flames stream into the

Opposite, above: The western Himalaya, a place of myth and legend through Indian history. Andrade's route into Tibet took him from Delhi to Hardwar, and over to Tsaparang; our detour led us through Jhang and Halji in the Limi valley. Opposite, below: A simplified transcription of the section of Father Monserrate's map of *c.* 1580 that first depicted the region of Lake Manasarovar. Until that point nothing was known of the interior of Tibet.

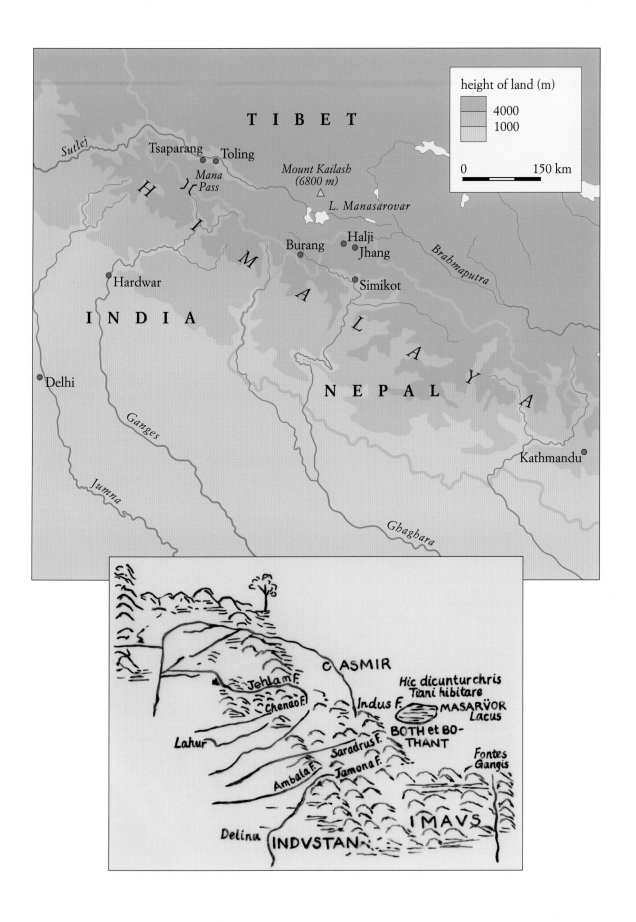

TIBET

Sutlej

Tsaparang Toling

Mana Pass

Mount Kailash (6800 m) △

L. Manasarovar

Burang Halji
Jhang

Simikot

Hardwar

INDIA

Brahmaputra

H I M A L A Y A

Delhi

NEPAL

Ganges

Jumna

Kathmandu

Ghaghara

height of land (m)

4000
1000

0   150 km

C·ASMIR

Jehlam F.

Hic dicunturchris
Tiani hibitare

Chenao F.

Indus F.

MASARÏOR
Lacus

Lahur

BOTH et BO-
THANT

Saradrus F.

Fontes
Gangis

Ambala F.

Jamona F.

Delinu **INDVSTAN**

I M A V S

night air, gilding the faces of pilgrims, and spangling the water, while the pilgrims sing their age-old hymns to Mother Ganga. Andrade was perhaps the first Westerner to see such things from the inside, though in the account written later for his superiors he finds it very difficult to escape the prejudices of his own time towards non-Western religions, and he dismisses the dreadlocked holy men as devil worshippers.

From Hardwar a footpath led right up into the Himalayas, as it still does. Andrade went in April, when the snow melts around the shrine at Badrinath. We followed in his footsteps through Rishikesh, where the Beatles came in the 1960s (those far-off days of innocence!). From here four hundred years ago the journey became a bigger ordeal. The caravan passed through Srinagar, in Garhwal, where the Europeans were arrested as spies, jailed and interrogated by the local rajah, but they were able to talk their way out. Beyond the valley of Srinagar the road climbs up to over 3000 metres through scented pine forests and thickets of lemon, juniper and rhododendron. From the modern road the old path taken by these early travellers can still be made out, scratched along beetling mountainsides, bearing out Andrade's vivid descriptions of terrifying drops, where the path is so narrow that one may 'only place one foot at a time', and sometimes has to 'cling for dear life to the rock face'. His story is echoed by other explorers who came after him on this same path: the Britons William Webb, in 1808, and Moorcroft and Hearsey, in 1812.

Finally at Joshimath the traveller is confronted by a wall of giant snow peaks, below which the river rushes down though steep gorges. This area is one of the holiest parts of India's sacred landscape because this is where the sacred river Ganges rises. Though fed by several tributaries, the Ganges has two main sources: at Gangotri, a wonderful spot where the water emerges from the foot of a glacier; and above Badrinath, where the river Alaknanda flows down from the mountains under snow-covered ranges. In between these two places are some of the most famous Himalayan shrines: the Shiva temple at Kedarnath, the cave at Amarnath with its lingam of ice, and Badrinath itself, which stands over hot springs in the middle of an icy desolation.

Andrade and his companion, the first Europeans to see these things, still thought they were going to find some kind of forgotten Christian world beyond the peaks. Strange as this may seem now, it is as well to remember that Buddhism had

Previous pages: Standing on the holy river Ganges, Hardwar is one of India's sacred cities – a paradise on earth to the pilgrims who gather there at festival time.

vanished in India long before their time. The religion which had begun in India in the sixth century BC and spread all over East Asia, had disappeared in India in the early Middle Ages, caught between Hindu revival and Muslim incursions. In the eighteenth century, when British orientalists, following clues from the Buddhist texts, struggled through the forests of Bodh Gaya and Nalanda to find the overgrown remains of huge Buddhist universities and monasteries, they had no idea that these had belonged to a great world religion which had originated in India, so completely had the Buddhist civilization of northern India been forgotten. No wonder then that in the sixteenth century, when rumours of a kingdom in western Tibet first reached the Moghul court, its rituals were compared to those of the Christians. The fact was, few people in sixteenth-century India had seen a Buddhist – or knew what one was.

INTO NEPAL

We followed Andrade's route by jeep into the Himalayas as far as it was possible to go; past the windswept and deserted pilgrim town of Badrinath and on to the point where the vehicle track ends, at Mana, the last village in India, which was empty now with winter coming on. There the military prevented us going any further. This was where Webb's expedition turned back in 1808: 'Ahead lay a fearful wall of ice,' he wrote. 'Our guides told us that beyond the peaks lay a city built by giants. And they refused to go any further saying that we could do so on our own – if we wished to be turned into stone.'

Used for centuries by pilgrims and traders, the walking path goes on up into the peaks for another 30 kilometres to cross the Mana Pass at over 5500 metres. High as it is, this was a main route into Tibet until 1950 when the Chinese occupied Tibet. Since then this ancient route, the one taken by Andrade and other early seekers and explorers, several of them British, has been closed to all travellers. In order to rejoin Andrade's track inside Tibet on the other side of the Himalayas, we were now forced to make an immense detour, to return to Delhi and fly to Kathmandu hoping to get behind the Mana Pass through western Nepal.

So, after our magical night of the full moon in Kathmandu, we began our journey to the west in a fifteen-seater light plane, fittingly owned by Shangri-La Airways. For a long while we flew along the Himalayas with sublime views of the peaks in the early sunlight: a slow procession past Annapurna and Manaslu – distant plumes of snow from the pyramid of Daulagiri trailing away in the jet stream.

Two days and another plane journey later we reached the little town of Simikot in the far west of Nepal. The landing strip is a dusty field on the edge of a ravine, overlooking gorges which sweep a thousand metres down to the ice blue of the Karnali river. Brushing the treetops, swooping down into the valley, the plane seemed for a moment to be aiming straight at a precipice, but sweeping over its lip we came to a jolting halt in cloud of dust. This was as far as Shangri-La Airways could take us.

Above us were mountains covered with thick conifer forests, their peaks flecked with snow. Machine-gun posts stood on the bluffs around us. War is in the air here. An old trading halt on the route to China, Simikot is now a government outpost surrounded by Maoist guerrillas who have most of western Nepal under

their control; to travel in this region you need to evade the government and pay off the guerrillas. Here there's a ruined fort, a few shops and a cluster of village houses built in the typical Humla style of rubble, mud brick and timber, all spread over a sunny hillside above the Karnali gorge.

Simikot has always been used by pilgrims, traders and herders moving between the plains of India and the high plateau. Caravans of sheep or yaks bring Tibetan salt down, and take back to the north red rice and barley, or white and black wool and timber from the Terai, the steamy subtropical lowlands of Nepal.

Opposite: Our journey westwards along the Himalayas and (above) our arrival at Simikot, fittingly on Shangri-La Air!

Watching them, I was reminded of Kipling's *Kim,* and the horse trader Mahbub Ali with his chain of contacts as far as Central Asia: the Tibetan traders and pilgrims who came down to the plains of India. Kipling, of course, was a journalist who knew at first hand the interaction of mountain and plateau people with people of the plains, and was familiar with the wandering monks from the region of frozen lakes on the edge of the high plateau. This world of transhumant herders, salt and yak caravans, bowl-makers, lamas and shamans still survives; and we hoped to be able to touch on it in the isolated valleys in the days ahead.

SNOW LEOPARDS AND DEMONS

There are many obstacles, physical and spiritual, which lie on the way to Shambala. But the seeker must also have the proper guide, for usually the knowledge of the right path is passed on orally in secret by one who has already made the journey …

The hostel hut has a wood-fired stove, and after dark we cook noodles and share a tot of brandy. Our guide, Tsewang lama, is a local wheeler-dealer, trader and sometime parliamentary representative. He's a Tibetan speaker from an old Buddhist family of lamas and gurus: his grandfather, 'a practitioner of good magic', was one of the most famous magicians in western Tibet before the Second World War. Tsewang, then, is a man who moves between two worlds, both the physical and the imaginal – a useful ability on such a journey.

That first night Tsewang told us more of the people of these lonely valleys, the 'non-caste people' (Tibetans) and 'caste people', as he called them – Hindus of Indian stock, dark skinned, with rings in their noses. Up here in this remote corner the people are mainly Tibetan speakers, though in Nepal as a whole four-fifths of the population are Hindu. So we are in a borderland between worlds here, a fault line of cultures as pronounced as the geological barrier of the Himalayas; between the Hindu world of plains India and the Buddhist and shamanistic religions of the high Tibetan plateau.

That night by the stove in the village hostel I spread out a map and Tsewang talked about the road ahead. The main route west to the border crossing at Burang was blocked by the Maoist guerrillas. However, his local contacts said there were no Maoists in the Limi valley, the furthest valley in Nepal, and the one where

---

Previous pages: Simikot, an ancient trading post in the Karnali gorge. The old route to Lake Manasarovar leads up to the horizon on the left.

Tibetan culture has survived in its purest form. Limi was reachable by supply helicopter, which on payment could detour and drop us off. From there Tsewang and his friends could take us to China on foot within a week.

Tsewang is a great story-teller and soon abandoned my literal map for a much more allusive one. He told us about the custom of polyandry in the villages out here, in which one woman often marries two or three brothers. He told us too of the persistence of the old spirit world, the demons. Not so long ago three snow leopards had been found inside a village house but, though surrounded by guns and traps, had somehow leapt out of a window and escaped: 'Everyone in the village believed they were demons.'

And he also talked of Shambala. We were now, he said, inside the mandala, the sacred zone of Kailash, the holy mountain. In traditional belief Kailash is surrounded by a ring of subsidiary peaks – twenty-one of them – just as in the legend of Shambala. In the old picture of the universe Kailash is at the centre. 'My father believed in a flat earth. He taught me that Kailash is the earthly mani-festation of the celestial Mount Meru and is at the centre of the universe. I have never argued with him about this and I have never attempted to dissuade him from his opinions about the cosmos. That would not be respectful.'

He smiled: 'In a sense he is happier than me. You see, to be born into the traditional world and then move into yours is not easy. I had psychological problems when I was young, caught between the two worlds.'

He raked the fire, and the sweet-scented resin in the pine logs bubbled and hissed. 'Go too far into the new and it is impossible to go back to the old. You carry with you the seed of a different knowledge, and you cannot stop it growing inside you. It gnaws at the security of the old mind of former times.'

As if to dismiss the thought, Tsewang came back to scrutinize my map again. He drew his finger down our route to China. 'We will land in Limi, walk through Jhang, Halji and Til, then to China. In this valley you will see the old culture of Tibet still alive.'

He told us about the characters we might meet en route: Ngari horsemen in their blue coats; Nepali shamans in white pants and jackets and hats of white wool, with great chillums of hashish to smooth the way into their trances; Indian sadhus in saffron with trident and bell; and the Chinese border soldiers in their baggy green fatigues. 'The People's Army are very strange human beings,' he said. 'A peculiar thing has happened to them when you look into their eyes. It is as if something has been cut away from them. They come from a purely materialist world. Some of them seem to be human beings with no soul.'

The fire was almost out. I was nodding off now, dreaming of fields of amaranth and roses, turbanned shamans with skulls and pistols. It was time to turn in. In the early hours I woke up suffering from altitude and dehydration, my mind in an eerie reverse playback, looping on the same scene, like an opium fizz. Stumbling to the tap outside, I gulped icy water under a starry sky and finally fell asleep, snow leopards in my dreams flying over frozen hills and frosted forests, leaving the soft print of their paws in the pale drifts.

THE FLIGHT TO LIMI

The helicopter skims the saddle of the mountains so closely that I instinctively brace myself as we seem to brush the tops of the pine forests at 3000 metres. In the early light, the sun is still not on the valley floor. We are travelling with the Nepal Trust, who are dropping medical supplies, bales of cotton, and gleaming sheets of corrugated iron into the Limi valley. There they will drop us too. Below us the blue ribbon of the Karnali snakes under thick pine forests, broken by the occasional patchwork of terraces in the middle of nowhere. Gorges seamed with snow run up on the left-hand side to the peaks of western Nepal, revealing a wonderful view of the summit of Saipal. Suddenly the river gorge veers right, and the pilot follows, swinging due north; briefly we have a distant glimpse into Tibet, and in a few moments we are coming down into the Limi gorge. Soon the landscape opens out to reveal neatly ordered wheat fields cut with streams and water channels, and small waterwheels. Then, set back in the side of the valley, under the gleaming lip of a glacier, we glimpse a small and perfectly preserved medieval walled town. Houses of drystone walls, the same grey colour as the mountain, cluster round a red-painted monastery, sunlight glinting off the golden wheel of dharma on its roof and the bronze flagpole. Shards of blue sky flash in the irrigation streams as we make our descent. In the bright yellow fields are hundreds of black dots – yaks coming down from their summer pastures. To the right we can see now that the whole valley is enclosed by a pink wall of mani stones, with roofed chortens – Buddhist memorial archways – at the entrances. It is a scene from a fairy-tale.

Our Russian pilot makes a hasty search for a landing site and then comes down on a field on the edge of a broken ravine, great clouds of dust billowing as we touch down. In a civil war a helicopter is quite a prize, and our pilot is nervous about the guerrillas: he keeps his engine running as the engineer opens the back doors, dumps our tents and gear, and waves goodbye. Within minutes they are airborne again. A gale of grit and chaff swirls over us, beating into our eyes and mouths, as we watch the helicopter lift over the mountains and disappear. I turn to see sunburned villagers in felt coats and yakskin hats, grinning kids with apple-red faces. The last faint thud of rotor blades dies away, and the rush of the stream and the creak of a waterwheel come to the ears. Just so easily may one step from one world into another.

THE HIDDEN VALLEY

> Many centuries ago the great tantric master Padmasambhava designated twenty-one secret valleys in the Himalayas and rendered them invisible to provide hidden retreats for the faithful in times of danger. Each is to be used only when a specific crisis occurs and will remain closed until that time … Some scholars say Shambala is one of these; some say they are visible only to the highest kind of yogis; others say that such valleys do exist in reality – that they are the places where the enlightened take refuge and where sacred objects and texts are hidden away in times of danger to await rediscovery.

Our first nights in the hidden valley were spent in the village of Jhang, a three-hour trek from our landing site. We camped by an ice-blue stream, where a ghostly thicket of skeletal birch trees cloaked the far slopes, all silvery trunks and feathery branches. Across a golden stubble of harvested barley, the massive drystone walls of the houses towered like a castle, with long streamers of coloured prayer flags strung across the lanes and fluttering over the valley.

We had arrived at festival time. For the next three days the monastery would be the focus of entertainment, drama and ritual for the whole village, just as it has been for the last thousand years. The great yard was roofed with an enormous canopy which bucked and swayed in the wind; huge tattered black flags sewn with Tibetan script hung down the front of the prayer hall. People were crowded into the wooden galleries on all four sides, women and children upstairs, the men downstairs in all their finery: high boots, fancy waistcoats and breeches, gold-braided Tibetan hats, and long, purple, fur-lined coats. For the next three days they would watch ritual dances and stories, folk plays on Buddhist themes, interspersed

Overleaf: Heading up the Limi valley near Jhang, a remote outpost of traditional Tibetan culture inside modern Nepal.

with comic interludes. The dances were the most impressive: to the clash of cymbals and the blast of huge trumpets, the great figures of Tibetan Buddhist myth would spin across the yard in centuries-old silk costumes and huge lacquered masks with grinning teeth and bulging eyes. All this was washed down with an endless supply of yak butter tea, barley beer and cheap Chinese brandy. Tibetans, we soon learned, certainly like to party.

Before we left Jhang we went to see the lama – a big burly man with a fine old red silk coat. His family made us butter tea as he took us to the prayer room of his

Previous pages: Horse games at the village of Jhang at the time of the autumn festival.
Above: The lama of Jhang in his prayer room with a medieval bronze rescued from Toling in Tibet.

house to show us silk hangings, books and sculptures, as well as a fine bronze with its arms and legs hacked off. These treasures, he told us, had been saved from the wholesale destruction on the other side of the border during the Cultural Revolution, when the Chinese Red Guards had rampaged through western Tibet, wrecking all the shrines round Kailash and the sacred lake, and smashing the unique temples of Tsaparang. Here, out of the reach of prying eyes, were hundreds of manuscripts, some of them gilded, hidden in the upper storey of the house.

'Until the modern world this was always part of Tibet,' said Tsewang, 'and it is pure Tibetan in its culture. The accident of drawing up the border put them in Nepal, but their true allegiance is not to a modern state but to the old monastic culture of Tibet. It's been destroyed on the other side,' he added, 'but here it's still alive.'

Standing in the lama's house it struck me how like the legends this was: a hidden valley; a monastery saving the wisdom of the ancients after the catastrophe, and handing it on to the future. Before I left I told the lama about the tale of Shangri-La.

'It still exists,' he said.

THE RED MONASTERY

On our third day in the valley, we set off with pack animals towards China. It was mid-November, and winter was coming on now. The herds were coming down from the summer pastures, and the lama of Jhang sent us on with a caravan of yak herders heading the same way, with children, old women, and men burned black by the sun. The women walked with baskets on their backs held by a forehead band – baskets containing blackened cooking pots, firewood, water bottles, old rugs. Usually they only come back home for three months each year, and sometimes they even winter on the summer pastures. It is a very hard life, and they are very tough people. For centuries, maybe for thousands of years, they have made this journey up to the plateau of Tibet to graze their animals. Now since the 1960s the border has been closed. Nomads don't count in the world of international diplomacy, of bureaucrats in their ministries. So now they can no longer keep such big herds, their livelihood is in tatters. Up here the ancient world is hanging on by its fingertips.

We reached the approaches to Halji in the mid-afternoon. By then the wind was blowing quite a gale, and dust was whipping into our faces, as forty or so mounted men came up on caparisoned horses, two of them bearing tattered

standards, like the last remnant of the army of Genghis Khan. They had brought spare mounts, and we rode on with them to the point where the valley narrows, and the river curves away round a ridge of glacial morrain which cuts across the valley bottom. We urged our horses up on to the ridge and followed the standards under a pink chorten at the top, a ceremonial gateway whose wooden roof was painted with scenes from the life of the Buddha. Once through the chorten a wonderful view opened out: we gazed at a patchwork of barley fields, golden and yellow-brown with winter coming on, criss-crossed by a filigree of water channels, and dotted with big herds of yaks and goats. Ahead of us the town stood on a low hill underneath brown crags, which were topped by the thick white edge of a glacier like a dazzling layer of white icing.

We rode on towards the town along a pink wall of mani stones carved with prayers and mantras, the boundary of the sacred precinct. Soon the huge building of the monastery loomed above us, whitewashed and with a thick band of red ochre under the eaves. Such a splendid vision made us rub our eyes, especially as a huge gust of wind suddenly stirred up a dust storm and for a moment wiped the whole picture away. At the gate two or three hundred people crowded around us, and we stopped and dismounted to meet the monks in their red gowns; above us glinting in the sun was the gilded wheel of dharma, attended by deer – for even animals must listen to the Buddha's message of compassion. As we entered, a yak was slaughtered, in preparation for the feast, and dismembered on the killing stone by the gate, splashing the ground with blood. And so, in a scene from another time, we arrived at the monastic town of Halji.

THE LORD OF DEATH

The valley's sides are steep and the sun disappears by 4 o'clock, leaving a cold twilight with a translucent sky; by 5.30 it's pitch-dark. After nightfall when the moon comes up the thick ice of the glacier glows an unearthly blue-white below a sky full of stars. From the monastery comes the sound of trumpets and the great drum. That night we took our places as special guests in the yard, with an unending supply of tsampa (white barley flour mixed with water), along with hot tea made with rancid yak butter, and chang (cold barley beer).

That night the monks told us the story of the monastery. It was founded in the

Opposite: Our journey to Halji. Limi is still untouched by the car, and travelling on horseback and by foot are the main means of transport.

990s by King Yeshe Ö and his great scholar-translator Rinchen Zangpo. This was a talismanic moment in Tibetan history. Buddhism had triumphed in Tibet in the eighth and ninth centuries, evangelized by the holy man and miracle worker Milarepa, though the indigenous cult, known as Bon Po, survived alongside it, as it still does. At that time Buddhism became the state religion. But in the bitter civil wars of the ninth century, the kingdom of Tibet was split apart. One of the royal family then migrated to the far west, to the lonely valleys of the Karnali, where he founded a new kingdom, Guge. There, just over a thousand years ago, an astonishing and beautiful culture arose. The Guge kings attracted great figures from India at a time when Buddhism was dying there. A massive translation programme was undertaken to turn Indian texts into Tibetan; bronze-casters and sculptors from northern India plied their craft here; and the finest Kashmiri artists were enticed to come to Guge to decorate the walls of the monasteries. All in all 108 monasteries were founded from the mother house of the Guge kingdom, the monastery of Toling. Almost all were later destroyed, but Halji is a rare survival, and it has come down in an unbroken line of descent from the original mysterious kingdom of the west. As it happens, this was just the time when the legend first arose in India of a magical kingdom behind the Himalayas, a land of peace and wisdom: Shambala.

The Limi valley is cut off from the rest of Nepal by snow from late November till April. Once the yak and sheep herders come back from their summer pastures, the nights close in and there is nothing for it but barley beer and early to bed. The rituals and shows in the great yard are the only public entertainment, and all are expected to attend. Like a medieval town, Halji is ordered and controlled by the monks. The people practise a strict polyandrous marriage system, but there are still surplus men, many of whom go into the monastery: even today, in the tiny population of two or three hundred, there are still forty-five monks. Tonight they are sitting along the end wall with their bowls of tsampa, the abbot in the place of honour. This is one of the few remaining societies to be ruled by a monastic theocracy, and inhabitants who break the rules or misbehave are subject to stiff fines. As always in history, anywhere in the world, religion gives order and law, meaning and identity, but it also imposes chains, mental and physical.

Over the next two or three days we shared in the life of the town. We saw the monks singing in the prayer hall and making mandalas in the shape of Meru, the

Opposite: Spirit dances in the yard of the monastery at Halji. The wooden galleries reminded me of Elizabethan theatres; the costumes and masks are heirlooms that are sometimes centuries old.

cosmic mountain, which they offered to the altar with barley meal on silver dishes, to the sound of trumpets, conch shells and cymbals. In the courtyard we watched the slow and stately mask dance – a procession of fanged pigs, scaly elephants with devils' horns, and red demons ringed with skulls. But the central figure is from Indian myth: the figure of the Lord of Death himself, Yama Rajah or, as he is also known, Mahakala, 'The Great Time'. The Lord of Death has a flouncing gown and a great black mask, with dripping fangs, and a huge butcher's knife. Ancient ivory phylacteries dangle by his face, as he holds up to the audience's gaze a piece of human skull with a Buddhist sutra on it. His message: This is your karma, your

Above and opposite: The beautiful costumes of the unmarried women as they wait to perform their dance in the yard.

destiny. Whatever you are, king or pauper, you are under his domain. So do not forget dharma, the norms and values of life; for only by your good actions in this life can you hope to attain Buddhahood – release from the wheel of rebirth.

'In Western countries, you see, death is an accident,' said Tsewang, as we cupped our hands round steaming cups of yak tea to keep warm. 'You are unprepared, and it steals up on you. You are so ambitious, working so hard, gathering possessions, you don't know how or when it will come, and you live in fear of it. In Eastern countries, Buddhist lands, death is practised from the beginning: remember your death, help other people help the poor, be compassionate, share your wealth and accept from the beginning – don't be so ambitious.'

'I know what you mean,' I said. 'We always seem to live our lives in a permanent state of stress.'

He pursed his lips sympathetically: 'We have no word for stress in Tibetan.'

In Halji everyone agreed that they were still loyal to the old ways. But for how much longer? One old man told me: 'We are poor, and live a very hard life, but we are rich in our culture. We are isolated between Tibet and Nepal. Till three years ago people here had very little chance to meet outsiders like you. That process of change is now beginning.'

'But remember,' said the man next to him, resplendent in an old rust-red chuba and gold hat, 'Some people here have travelled to Kathmandu, even to Delhi, Dehra Dun and Kangra. They know of the outside world. We need electricity, hydroelectric power and telephone communications. Our grazing rights were given away in the first border negotiations with the Chinese in 1961, because the Nepali government was not serious about the rights of semi-nomadic peoples to move over borders. Now we desperately need new forms of livelihood, to feed ourselves and to save our culture. Now our summer pastures in China have been given away by some government man in Kathmandu we have no alternative. We have to be part of the modern world, because the modern world has taken away our traditional way of life. Sure we are rich in culture, but material needs must come first.'

And along with those, the agents of modernity no doubt will follow. Such is the dilemma of the real-life inhabitants of Shangri-La.

Opposite: A young man in the yard at Halji.
Overleaf: Crossing the Limi river on the way to Tibet. This path has been used for centuries by seasonal herders, salt caravans and itinerant bowl-makers.

TO THE BORDER

Next day we walked to Til, the last village before the border with Tibet. We began early, and had a wonderful walk through a sylvan meadow, with mountain juniper and birch stands glowing in autumn colours. We passed some travelling bowl-makers, a family with children and six horses coming down from China where they had sold their bowls to a dealer in Burang. Over tea they told us about their craft, and how the Limi valley dominates the trade with Tibet of these beautiful bowls, which are treasured in good homes and traditional families. For some bowls they use pine and birch, but the best quality ones are made in maple burl, which produces the characteristic whorls and patterns. To obtain this precious wood, six or seven times a year they walk down to Kumaon in India, coming back to Jhang for the winter. The old circulation of humanity!

Snowflakes were blowing into our faces in the late afternoon before we reached the turn-off to Til. The village is at the top of a dramatic valley below two immense black pinnacles, more than 6000 metres high, that stand out on the border with Tibet. Huge snowy shoulders drifted in and out of sight in a grey twilight world of mist, glaciers and snow-streaked crags, a forbidding vista which looked for all the world like the abode of the gods.

The last hour of our walk we trudged leaden-footed up a steep path in a bitter, sleety rain. Away to the right a tiny monastery nestled in a bleak ravine near the clouds, and Tsewang pointed out the crag where three Halji monks are fulfilling a vow of meditation which involves separation from the world for three years, three months and three days.

'There is the cave where they live,' he said. I peered through failing light speckled with snow, to a hole under a rock where a bent tree hung over a vertiginous drop.

'Two live there, one over the top. They have water. The monastery sends up food supplies every week or so.'

We pitch our tents by an icy stream in a frozen meadow, amid flurries of snowflakes. The river has a crust of ice, and the grass is crisp and white. Later we stagger into the village, dishevelled and chilled to the bone; after sunset it is cold, with winter really coming in. On hearing that we are heading for the holy mountain of Kailash, the headman makes a sweet speech with a traditional doxology: 'If there were no Kailash, then there would be no Manasarovar [the sacred lake], then no rivers, no irrigation, no barley, and no chang. And if there were no chang there would be no festivals for the gods, no dancing, no status, no society, no love, marrying and enjoyment of life. The chain of being here depends on the sacred mountain as it does on nature itself.'

The entertainment tonight in the monastery is not spirit dances but music, games and comic interludes performed by young men of the town; all under the beady eyes of the abbot, who sits in the place of honour. He sports a yellow and red sash across a silk robe, with a woolly hat and a rather incongruous badge at his forehead showing the guru of his sect in a tall red hat. With a face like a blackened walnut, and an impish expression, he is famous not as an administrator but as a meditation lama, renowned for his spiritual battles out in the wilds. 'He is the lama of the cave,' Tsewang whispers as we walk up to his table. 'As far as lamas go, he has done it all – and more.' That, I imagined, meant continuing the tradition of Milarepa and other heroes of the high plateau, who like the early Christian desert fathers conquered all desire and pain. We shake hands. On such a chill night, the monk's hands are warm.

It's late when we pick our way unsteadily down the steep path to the bridge over the river gorge and somehow find our tents. One of our group doesn't make it back to our frozen meadow, having had too much chang, and is put to bed by the women of the village. The villagers have been pressing us to stay longer, but we cannot. Our Tibetan friends who will take us to our final destination will already have set out on the six-day journey from Lhasa to meet us. In two days' time we must make our rendezvous with them on the Tibetan border.

We awoke to find our water bottles frozen solid in our tents. Outside my tent flap there was a white rime in the field, and a shell of ice on the river. But the snow had held off. The village was still sleeping after the party, and our departure was delayed by the lack of horses. Ahead of us was a journey of about seven hours, to our next campsite, starting with a long steady climb to the Lamka La Pass at about 4200 metres. As we struggled against a freezing wind, I found myself thinking again of the early travellers to western Tibet; especially of Antonio Andrade in 1624, sick from altitude, a finger gone from frostbite, with nothing to eat but tasteless barley meal. After the pass we gingerly negotiated a huge drop down a boulder-strewn waste. The path at times was single file, a faint scar across immense screes. The worst thing was the constant up and down – a couple of hundred metres climb, then down again. By dusk we were all dog-tired. On the last stage we skirted the Karnali gorge, where the massive brown roots of mountains rose up to the snow-line like giant claws before disappearing into the mists that occasionally lifted enough to reveal jagged peaks in the failing light. This was not an earthly geography, it seemed to me; more like the mountains of Mordor.

In pitch-dark we found our campsite, sheltered by some boulders on an open mountainside at 4000 metres, and lit a fire to make tea. Some of the horses arrived later that night with the tents, and we got a little sleep. At dawn we woke to find that the clouds had cleared to reveal a lovely crystal day. After a further stiff four-hour walk we at last caught sight of the tiny border settlement at Hilsa, and the new Chinese army post on a hill on the other side. Our new guide, Gyurme, had arrived the previous night and was waiting at the border with the Tibetan team and two jeeps. There was time only to unload the packhorses and say our goodbyes to Tsewang and our Nepali friends, who would walk all the way back to Simikot. As they made their way down to the river, we set off on the winding dirt road to Burang. Behind us the sunset along the Himalayan ridges was majestic. We had finally reached Tibet.

INTO TIBET

> The most sacred teaching of Shambala is called the Great Circle of Time. This teaching is of primeval origin, from long before the Buddha of history. It tells of a prophecy that one day humans by their greed and ignorance will ravage the very earth itself … But it also says that in time human beings will recognize that their passions are the chief cause of all their ills, and then the King of Shambala shall at last govern all mankind … and a Golden Age will come when wisdom will at last be enthroned on earth.

We check into the Pea Fowl Hotel, a decaying Chinese provincial hotel with no electricity, running water or working loos. But it will do: a real comfort after the last week's camping. Burang is something of a Wild West border town, and in the old days it commanded enough of a tradeway into India for the British to have appointed a resident here after the Younghusband expedition of 1904. Now the population is mainly police, army and customs, served by a few shops and restaurants, nightclubs, and a karaoke bar-cum-brothel for the Chinese troops. It is not, one imagines, the most sought-after posting. Across the stream are the Indian and Nepali bazaars, where the Limi traders sell their bowls and where the merchants of the sheep caravans barter grain for salt with the nomads. Now that cross-border traffic is over for the year, the bazaars are winding down. After 1949 this was a forbidden zone, and it has only slowly opened up in the last twenty years. Now, in the new world of Chinese tourism, cross-border links are growing. On a hill above the town are the ruins of Shimbling monastery, which had 170 monks up to the Second World War;

they controlled the salt trade with the nomads, who had to pay tribute to the monastery or risk being punished with sorcery. This was why one of the Humla salt-caravan chiefs brought Tsewang's grandfather, a famous magician, here from central Tibet to defend the nomads and release them from the spells. The monastery is finished now, and the monks are gone. The world of spells is vanishing.

THE LAKE AT THE CENTRE OF THE WORLD

As we leave Burang, in the early light there are wonderful vistas of the Indian Himalaya almost as far as Nanda Devi, the highest peak in India. We drive up a long, brown valley, denuded of all vegetation, dotted with small shrines and country houses painted red and white. Soon the great whaleback of Gurla Mandhata (7700 metres) rises on our right, its summit streaming long tails of snow, ice fields shining in the early sunlight. Then, at the Gurla Pass, by a cairn of mani stones heaped with prayer flags, we get our first view of the holy mountain. Kailash is still over 100 kilometres away, but its white summit gleams like a beacon over the brown plain. In front is the deep blue expanse of Rakshas Tal, demon lake, framed by barren, treeless shores, its ominous surface flecked by relentless winds. To the east we begin to see the dark sheen of Manasarovar, the sacred lake named on the 1580 map.

We cross the isthmus past Chiu Gompa and reach the shore of Manasarovar. The highest big freshwater lake in the world, Manasarovar was long viewed by pilgrims as the source of four of the great rivers of Asia – the Indus, Brahmaputra, Karnali and Sutlej – which all rise close by, and the Jumna and Ganges, not so far off. So it is an axial point which has drawn pilgrims for thousands of years – and still does. The region was closed to outsiders after 1949, and no foreign visitors came here till the early 1980s, when Indian pilgrims were allowed through in limited groups. Now it is on the pilgrim trail again.

The lake edge is solid with ice. Fifty metres out a row of stakes runs parallel to the shore, draped in frosted strings of prayer flags tattered by the wind: this is the marker line for pilgrims who come here in summer to take a sacred bath. Along the shore are traces of old campfires, and the frozen leftovers of pilgrimage. The far shore is 20 kilometres across the water; further away we can see the mountains of Humla, and 160 kilometres off the distinctive pinnacle of Daulagiri in a cloudless azure sky.

Overleaf: Mount Kailash, viewed from across the plains. Kailash is regarded by Hindus and Buddhists as an earthly manifestation of the celestial Mount Meru, the *axis mundi*. It is easy to see how the legend of a crystal mountain evolved.

Next day we visit Chiu Gompa, where there are no monks, but five priests who keep the prayers up. The little monastery has been restored since the Cultural Revolution, but had also known many previous destructions. In 1941 all the gompas around the lake were looted by Kazakh bandits from the Soviet empire, three thousand of whom rode on a great razzia through western Tibet, seizing cattle, looting and killing. A priest shows us a tiny cave below the prayer hall: this, he says, is where Padmasambhava meditated during his battles of the spirits in the ninth century. Padmasambhava, like Andrade and the Jesuits, was another missionary who came into an alien world, that of the old Tibetan religion of Bon Po, to convert the people and co-opt the old deities of the land, the gods of mountains and lakes. The heroic tale of the guru in his cave is, I suppose, a parable of the triumph of Buddhism in western Tibet. Thinking of the lama in Til, I comment to Gyurme on the physical toughness of the old monks, their capacity to withstand austerities.

'They must have been tough old birds.'

'It is not a matter of that,' he replies. 'Their minds had evolved on a plane we cannot begin to comprehend.'

Next morning, the late November light down by the lake shore is simply unearthly. As the sun rises, the colour of the water changes from deep indigo to an intense bright blue. Birds rise in silver flashes; a long V of migrating geese flies overhead; fresh-water dolphins break the surface. Along the lake shore the great shelf of ice, so thick you can walk on it, begins, as it is gradually warmed by the sun, to groan, creak, squeak and chatter; clacking and chirping, the noise grows like a flock of birds. It is as if the lake is alive with ghosts. (And indeed, in Tibetan belief the lake is a gateway to the subterranean world of demons, wraiths and serpent spirits.)

THE HOLY MOUNTAIN

For centuries the strange shape of Kailash, quite isolated from the rest of the Himalayan chain, has exerted a peculiar hold on the imagination. It is the perfect crystal pyramid – which was surely what Hilton had in mind when he described the sacred mountain in his fictional Shangri-La. In the old days the Nepali sheep herders, and sellers of rice and wool, would seal their deals with oaths of

Previous pages: Chiu Gompa, a tiny monastery on the shore of Lake Manasarovar, in the wonderful clarity of late November light on the high plateau of Tibet.
Opposite: Mount Kailash, seen from the entrance to the great western canyon. Sacred for millennia to Hindus, Buddhists, Jains and followers of the indigenous Bon Po religion of Tibet, no mountain in the world is more cloaked in myth.

friendship, a shared plate of rice shaped like the holy mountain, and a container of water to signify the sacred lake Manasarovar: bonds of commerce sworn on a replica of the crystal mountain at the centre of the universe. The mountain was almost a living presence.

Pilgrimages to Kailash stopped in 1949 and, after the destruction of the holy sites around it in the Cultural Revolution, only began again with a trickle of intrepid travellers in the early 1980s. Prior to the twentieth century it was one of the loneliest places in the world. The first outsider who we know saw it was the Italian Desideri in 1715. He was awestruck. 'In this vast, terrible and sterile desert,' he wrote, 'stands a huge mountain always enveloped in cloud, covered with snow and ice, and truly horrible, barren, steep and bitterly cold …' Rubbing his eyes with snow to ease his snow blindness Desideri listened to tales of the great yogis Milarepa and Padmasambhava with their supernatural feats. He also heard how the local people 'devoutly walk round the base of the mountain, which takes several days, and they believe gives them great benefits'. For a long time outside visitors were few and far between. The next we know of was William Moorcroft in 1812. A Lancastrian surgeon, Moorcroft lived a life of extraordinarily eccentric adventure, apparently dying in Balkh, although strange rumours circulated long afterwards that he had swapped his identity, gone native and ended his days somewhere out here in the zone of the sacred mountain.

The Kailash range rises dark grey, straight out of the yellow plain above which the snow-capped pyramid gleams eerily; clearly visible on its south face are the strange black horizontal scars that gave rise to one of its many names: 'the nine-storey swastika mountain'. To the Bon Po, Jains, Buddhists and Hindus, to so many of the peoples of Asia, this is the central place, represented in art and myth for thousands of years. To Hindus, it is the dwelling place of the great God Shiva, and is often equated with both Mount Meru, the imaginary mountain at the centre of the universe in Hindu mythology, and with the crystal mountain by the lotus lake in the Tibetan Shambala myth. As mountains go, Everest may be higher, but in the mythic stakes Kailash takes all prizes.

The pilgrimage to Kailash involves a 50-kilometre circuit, which is done on foot, sometimes with prostration at every step. The sacred path leads from the plain into the beautiful canyons of the western valley and on to the haunting spectacle of the icy north face. Rising a sheer 2000 metres in front of your eyes, like a giant snow-streaked black crystal, this primordial mass was formed in the depths of the primal ocean tens of millions of years before the rising of the Himalayas: though the pilgrims may not know it, Kailash really does represent an older order of time. With some of the greatest rivers of Asia flowing away from this mandala in four different directions, it is not difficult to see how this place has come to be seen as unique on the face of the earth, the sum of all journeys.

Darchen is our stop for the next couple of days. It is a shabby frontier town hemmed in by a squat and ugly military camp with half-finished concrete perimeter walls. Our hotel is owned by the local police, who have woken up to the fact that there is money to be made out of the magic mountain. The province of Ngari has only opened up in the last twenty years, and travellers still need a special permit to be here. However, as more and more Himalayan lands become problematical – al-Qaeda in Pakistan, separatists in Kashmir, Maoists in Nepal – Tibet, for so long the forbidden land, now beckons invitingly. An airport is being constructed in the west, and a new road past Kailash to Burang will link up with a new land route into India. The most difficult and demanding pilgrimage on earth will suddenly be within reach of package tours.

But not quite yet. At least for now the sacred centre is still at the outer limits of travel. The town itself is just a collection of mud-brick shanties and tents, with stalls mainly run by Khampas from the east. It is they who give the place its Wild West feel: with their sunburned faces they look like North American Indians, but they have all the macho swagger of cowboys. Swathed in big, fur-lined gowns of grey wool tied with a length of old rope or an old money belt, they strut around in battered, high-heeled riding boots, their long hair wound in red braid and set off by large gold and turquoise earrings. Their long knives dangling in silver scabbards, they patrol outside their tented shops selling Lhasa beer, chocolate, batteries, baseball hats, music cassettes and bags of the mountain herb (zhang ze) much valued by Tibetans for burning in their rituals. Watching them with their wide, knowing smiles as they finger their daggers, it is easy to believe the old stories about pilgrims' caravans being robbed by brigands. My 1949 guidebook to Kailash warns the traveller against bandits on the road. They are still here.

In the afternoon we go out to the western valley to visit the site of the great flagpole which is set up each year for the festival at the summer solstice. The place is at the mouth of a canyon whose brown buttresses guard the inner fastnesses of the range. It is quite empty now, with not a soul in view, and the only sound is that of flags flapping in the wind. Near the pole are big heaps of offerings: mani stones, yak horns and, again, carvings of Meru, the divine lotus mountain of which Kailash is the earthly manifestation. Towering above us, and dazzling white in the sun, the peak itself seems close enough to touch, every detail of its face distinguishable, though it is 16 kilometres away. Sadly, close as we are, we have no time to walk the

circuit now, up to the snow and ice of the Dolma Pass, at 5800 metres, and the fantastic vistas of the north face. The weather could turn any day; and pilgrimage, as the lamas say, is a thing to be done at the right time and the right pace. For now, simply to see such a magnificent spectacle of nature so close, and on such a brilliant end-of-year day, is quite enough.

THE JOURNEY TO THE LOST CITY

The next day we left Darchen and set out for the west, on the last leg of our journey to trace that of Antonio Andrade, the first Westerner to enter Tibet, and the first to see the mysterious kingdom of Guge. His crossing directly over the Himalayas from Mana had been an ordeal. He suffered from agonizing frostbite, and survived on tsampa, the dull barley meal which, if wood could be found, was cooked as chewy, tasteless pancakes. In a wool cloak and pilgrim's clothes, Andrade only just bore the cold, and by the end his feet were in a terrible state: at one point he had his wounds cauterized by his guides with a hot iron – though he was too far gone to feel anything. His route led over the Mana Pass on to the Tibetan plateau, where the Sutlej river, which rises on the west side of the Kailash massif, flows down into a weird landscape of immense eroded canyons. This was the heartland of the mysterious Guge kingdom, and this still little-explored tract of land was our final goal.

The last stage of our journey was a 400-kilometre drive westwards from Kailash on dirt roads as far as the ravine of the river Sutlej. This would take us along the back of the Himalayas to the very point where the seventeenth-century travellers (and their nineteenth-century successors) came into Tibet, and then on to the ruins of the lost medieval kingdom of western Tibet which first came to the notice of Westerners back in the days of Emperor Akbar.

On the way we stopped for a picnic lunch on the upper Sutlej at Tirthapuri. This is an Indian name – it is the most northerly site in the sacred geography of India. The guidebooks recommend pilgrims with time on their hands to take the hot springs here after doing the circuit of Kailash. In the old days there was a monastery which was sacked by Kazakh bandits during the attacks of 1941. Ruined again in the Cultural Revolution, it was never rebuilt, and now there is just a small mud-brick hostel for pilgrims. Around the site plumes of sulphurous steam rise

---

Opposite: Prayer flags at the great flagpole, where the annual Kailash summer pilgrimage begins. In the foreground is a heap of mani stones carved by pilgrims who have completed the arduous circuit.

from the hot springs, which in several places have made holes big enough for several people to sit in. We tore off our hiking boots and clothes and plunged in. After our weeks of footslogging it was simply fabulous.

For the rest of the day we journeyed over wide, wintry grasslands, passing only herds of gazelle and wild ass. We crossed rivers of ice, and traversed hills of brown, orange, rust-red and cuprous green, as if the landscape was made of decaying metals. Climbing higher now, we mounted a great escarpment of about 5000 metres, and then in the late afternoon came to an astonishing point where we could almost look down on the back of the Himalayas, from Humla in Nepal to the east to Zanskar and Ladakh in the west: a 650-kilometre panorama. Directly in front of us was the Indian Himalaya: Nanda Devi and the holy peaks around Joshimath, Gangotri and Badrinath, with the grasslands of the Tibetan plateau reaching right up to the foot of the glaciers. And there, shadowed in the late sun, we could see the place where the seventeenth-century travellers had crossed. Only 65 kilometres off, it looked as though we could have just strolled down and walked over into India.

Night was coming on, and we had to tear ourselves away from that splendid scene. The canyons of the Sutlej now came into view, stretching towards the sunset as far as the eye could see. The entry point was almost like a secret doorway: we suddenly passed through a gap in the mud cliffs strung with prayer flags, then began a winding descent into the bottom of the canyon. The landscape has been eroded into fantastic shapes by wind, rain and winter torrents, and in the half-light we saw what looked like huge columns and buttresses which seemed to belong to giants' castles, with towers and curtain walls, as every curve opened up a new vista. Then, after nearly an hour, the ravines opened out into a wide valley between cliffs, at the bottom of which the river Sutlej glinted in the last light. On a plateau across the valley we saw the lights of a signals mast: Toling, the final Chinese military base before the mountain passes.

It was dark before we reached the town, which serves as an army base, police post and radio station, with its street of shops and the inevitable nightclub for the Chinese troops. The famous monastery here, founded in 996, was one of the victims of the devastation of the 1960s. At the centre of this great complex was the temple of Yeshe Ö: a three-dimensional mandala with a central hall and eighteen subsidiary chapels, which made this one of the most ravishing buildings in Asia, a memory

---

Opposite: Our descent towards the Sutlej canyons, in the middle distance, with the Indian Himalaya on the horizon. No wonder the Guge kingdom remained isolated for so long and unknown to the wider world until the seventeenth century.

room of Tibetan culture. When you stepped out of the sunlight you entered a labyrinth full of magnificent bronzes, giant Buddhas and bodhisattvas, painted and gilded, and a wonderful cycle of medieval wall paintings: in sum, a literal representation of the world of the spirits. Now it's all gone, the images having all been smashed and dismembered. All we have left are a few precious photographs taken in the 1940s, and some inventories 'setting down in writing everything that was here, to make it easier for future ages to understand …' The 1870 inventory is eerily prophetic, uncannily prefiguring the myth we have been pursuing. This after all was the greatest monastery in the kingdom of the west – one could almost say the mother house of Shambala/Shangri-La in the last days of its existence:

> The times are bad. In the long run the images and the vessels and the property, large and small, will eventually be taken away. Since then there will be no chance of retrieving them, it will surely happen that one day in the future there will be nothing virtuous left outside and inside the monastery, in any place, and it will be like an empty paradise …

THE LOST CITY OF THE WEST

The Guge king had heard of the approach of the strangers, and for the last three days of his journey Andrade was accompanied by the king's servants, who had met him with horses and supplies. Andrade is curiously silent on that first encounter by a European. Not so Govinda, the last outsider to visit the Guge capital of Tsaparang before the fall, who saw its monasteries intact on the eve of the Chinese take-over:

> When we set eyes on the lofty castles of the ancient city of Tsaparang, which seemed to be carved out of the solid rock of an isolated monolithic mountain peak, we gasped with wonder and could hardly believe our eyes. In the great solitude and stillness of the abandoned city and in the mysterious semi-darkness of its temple-halls, the spiritual experiences and achievements of countless generations seemed to be projected into the magic forms of images. The temples seemed to be lifted out of the stream of time.

Opposite: Exterior walls of the mandala temple of King Yeshe Ö at Toling, the mother monastery of the Guge kingdom. Founded in 996, this was perhaps one of the models behind the lamasery in the modern legend of Shangri-La.

The city lies only 25 kilometres down the Sutlej valley from Toling. A giant beehive towering on a crag of sandstone and alluvial mud, the place is pockmarked with hundreds of caves. In the valley floor below are the remains of the buildings of the city, crumpled walls and stupas, melted by the rains, scattering the hillsides with clay offering-tablets stamped with sacred images. Among the few buildings that have been preserved is the royal palace of the Guge kings perched on the top of the citadel and reached through a warren of tunnels and passages. This is where Andrade arrived in August 1624 after his epic journey over the Himalayas: 'The people of the city came out, crowding every balcony,' he wrote, 'as if we were strangers from another world …'

The magnificent temples which Andrade saw in 1624 still survive, though many of their images were irretrievably damaged during the Cultural Revolution. The interior walls were once lined with huge plaster figures of Buddhist deities, painted and gilded, with metal aureoles; all were smashed save for one exquisite three-faced female deity, so lovely that one wonders whether some Red Guard couldn't bring himself or herself to wield the hammer. The wall paintings, however, did survive. For some reason the guards feared them less than the three-dimensional images and spared the sensational series of murals.

One of these, in the Red Temple, is a cycle of Kashmiri-style paintings done with incredible finesse and delicacy – perhaps by Indian artists – with gorgeous, intricate lush leaf ornament. There are scenes from the life of the Buddha and fascinating images showing the royal family of Guge, with their children, servants and musicians, at a festivity for the dedication of the temple: poignant snapshots from the enchanted life of the kingdom in the fifteenth century – a world stopped in time. Another haunting cycle in luscious deep reds and greens shows the tantric gods and goddesses, wrathful and benign.

Our guide Gyurme was visibly moved. A lifetime engaging with the story of Tibet does not, I imagine, lessen the feeling of desolation when faced with the reality of the loss. He sat down on a temple bench: 'These, remember, are meditational deities,' he began, 'only emanations of the human imagination.' He spoke for a while about the bardos, the uniquely Tibetan conception of birth, life and death as a series of intermediate stages which include the waking life, the state of dreams, and the after-death state when a hundred peaceful and wrathful deities emerge from the

Opposite: Tsaparang, the last capital of the lost kingdom of Guge, with the royal palace perched on top. Founded in the ninth century, the city was finally destroyed in 1685.

heart and brain to confront the deceased. 'These are the images around the walls. In death, it is important that they are recognized for what they are. These represent the purified nature of our being – they are, one might say, the building blocks of the world. But they are still only the products of our imagination.'

To us, of course, it is obvious that this culture is Buddhist. Andrade himself did not see this at first. Indeed, it was only after some time that he came to understand that the city's religion was not some long-lost Christian cult. Even then, Andrade remained unsure whether similarities with Christian ritual and imagery might not be due to some ancient contact or conversion of which no record survived. If he was disappointed, however, he didn't show it. He talked at length to the king and queen about the Christian faith. The king was so impressed by his passionate advocacy that he allowed Andrade to build a church there.

Opposite: One of the very few pieces of statuary to survive the wanton destruction of Tsaparang's temples in the Chinese Cultural Revolution of the 1960s.
Above: Fifteenth-century wall paintings from Tsaparang – exquisite but fragile reminders of a lost world.

Andrade had high hopes for his Tibet mission. Tibetans, he wrote, were 'good, honest, open-hearted people' who were ripe for conversion. With that in mind he returned to India and came back in 1625. But the mission was doomed to failure. Before he could undertake a third visit Andrade died mysteriously in India, of poison it was rumoured. The mission staggered on till the 1640s, after which there is no record of it. The last trace, the wooden cross of Andrade's little church, was seen by a traveller in 1912.

For Tsaparang the arrival of the first Westerners was the beginning of the end after nearly 700 years. Within a few years the neighbouring Buddhist king of Ladakh (who had long had contact with Guge over the mountain passes) opened hostilities against the kingdom – partly, it was said, because it had allowed foreigners in. The city survived a siege in the 1640s but not long afterwards came the dénouement – the fateful last siege of 1685, when the Ladakhis marched up the Sutlej valley with an army of Muslim mercenaries. A giant rubble siege tower, still to be seen today, was constructed to reach the citadel. The cause was hopeless and the king of Guge surrendered, believing he had been promised safe conduct. However, the king and his queen, together with their children and ministers, were beheaded in front of their people, and their heads were stuck on poles in front of the city gates. Even today, down a lonely gulley below the city walls, you will find a cave where the headless bodies of the royal family remain, in their shredded clothes, mummified in the dry climate. A macabre and tragic end to the magical kingdom.

Tsaparang and the great mother monastery of Toling are surely what Hilton had in mind when creating his fictional Shangri-La. The first photographs of the two places, published by Tucci in 1932, excited the world just as Hilton was planning his book. Hilton turns his lamasery into a more Western-style mixture of Christian and Buddhist with the 200-year-old Capuchin lama. But here, if anywhere, I tend to think, is the source of the Shangri-La story. Perhaps more important and interesting, the Guge kingdom may also have been the historical model for the mythical land of Shambala.

Our journey was over. We returned to Toling, and then over the next few days to Darchen and Burang. There we parted company with Gyurme and the boys from Lhasa, and scrambled down the hillside to the little bridge over the Karnali with our rucksacks and tent barrels. We were waved off by the young Chinese man in charge, a kindly and civilized officer: a man with a soul. We then recrossed the Nepali border to make our rendezvous with the supply helicopter from Nepalganj. We spent the last night of our expedition in tents on a little dusty plain by the river at Hilsa, before the helicopter came to lift us off and take us away. Back to our world.

EPILOGUE

We live in a time when the 'givenness' of the past is receding from us at an ever quicker rate, when all over the globe ancient identities are being rubbed away thoughtlessly, when the devastation of the environment and the extinction of species is causing growing alarm. The universal appeal of the tales of Shambala and Shangri-La I think connects with this (just as, for the same reason, the fate of Tibet itself has struck a chord everywhere). They are tales about our desire that something will remain, that our connection with our deep past should not be completely erased, even as we move faster and faster into an ever more uncertain future. The Tibetan lamas say that each of us can live in Shangri-La – if we can only conquer the restless need that makes us dream of paradises in worlds other than our own. James Hilton imagined Shangri-La in Tibet, but actual and potential Shangri-Las fill the world. Paradise can be found anywhere here on this earth – but only on this earth. It is in our hands whether we make it or destroy it. And perhaps that, ultimately, is the meaning of the myth?

> Before he left Shangri-La, Conway felt the surge of darkness around him, as if the world outside were already brewing for the storm … It was as if Shangri-La were a living essence, distilled from the magic of the ages and miraculously preserved against time and death …
>
> 'We have a dream and a vision,' the lama told him. 'The most beautiful things are transient and perishable: war, lust and brutality crush them till there is no more left in the world. That is why Shangri-La is here: to outlive the doom that gathers around on every side … to preserve the wisdom men will need when their violent passions are spent …

JAMES HILTON *Lost Horizon* 1933

JASON AND THE GOLDEN FLEECE

IT IS THE LAST HOUR BEFORE DAWN and the little island of Anafe on the southern edge of the Cyclades is still asleep. A place, and a moment, to imagine the world in the time of the Greek myths. The constellation of Orion stands out to the east below a waning moon, whose pale light shimmers on the sea. To the west there is still no separation of sky and earth, only the black shapes of islands rising out of the darkness. Down by the shore a faint breath of wind stirs the tamarisk trees along the beach. Then, to the east, the light begins, like that moment in the myths when, impregnated by the Wind, the goddess of Night lays a luminous egg in the womb of Darkness, and sets creation in motion. Ruffled by the rising breeze, the sea takes form and colour now, and islands emerge, recalling the ancient belief that all the gods and all living creatures were created in the stream of the Great Ocean which girdles the world.

Previous pages: Turkey's Black Sea coast, a dream of gold for the ancient Greeks. Above: Jason escapes from the dragon's mouth, apparently alluding to an otherwise unknown version of the myth.

In the earliest time in Greek myth, the time before Homer and the early epic poets, the extent of the world was a mystery and the shores of the Great Ocean bounded an infinite unknown. To the Greeks, what lay beyond the Mediterranean Sea was a land of the imagination rather than of physical reality. The first exploration of the shore of the Great Ocean, as far as the land where the sun rises, took place in the Heroic Age, before the Trojan War, and it ended here on Anafe. This was the expedition of Jason and the Argonauts, who sailed from Greece across the Black Sea to the far-off land of Colchis, today's Georgia, to find the mythical Golden Fleece. It is a fairy-tale of heroes and princesses, dragons and magic. It is a journey to the land of death which takes us inwards into the dark corners of the human psyche. But, real or imagined, it is also a sailors' story: the tale of a sea voyage, of a bid to explore beyond the edge of the known world, or, as a modern version of the myth puts it, 'to boldly go where man has never been before'.

THE LEGEND OF ANAFE

In Anafe, autumn is approaching and the brief tourist season that started in June has already come to an end. The warm summer wind from Africa has given way to the *meltemi*, which swirls from the north down the whitewashed alleys of the village, scouring the mountainsides and whipping up white caps in the little harbour. At this time the island communities gather themselves in and turn back to the old ways.

Here on the night of 6 September a procession climbs a precipitous cliff at the end of the island, where a lonely chapel hangs 500 metres above the sea. Carrying lanterns on poles, old ladies in black shuffle over the screes, mules pick their way, loaded with food and blankets, and black-capped priests hold banners and a miraculous icon. On top of the cliff, in a ritual far older than Christianity, they keep the vigil and greet the dawn. Later, back down below, they will bless and kill a sheep and eat a meal together in the monastery: the kind of open-air communal feast celebrated for millennia here in Greece.

The monastery on Anafe was built in the 1830s inside an ancient temple of Apollo: the huge ashlar blocks of the ancient sanctum became the refectory of the monks. The monks are gone now but a legend is still told about the place by the priest who supervises the festival.

After their many adventures on the long journey back from Colchis – the land of the rising sun – bearing the Golden Fleece, Jason and the Argonauts were swept

up by a terrifying storm in their boat, the *Argo*. As sky and sea merged in a fearful darkness, Jason prayed to Apollo, and the god, hearing his prayer, made an island suddenly appear in front of them, where the exhausted Argonauts were able to find dry land. This island, so the legend goes, was called Anafe, Greek for 'the one which was revealed'. And here, in thanks, they built a shrine dedicated to Apollo, 'the great healer', above the spot where they landed. This place is now occupied by the Christian monastery.

The legend of Anafe is first recorded by Apollonius of Rhodes in the third century BC. According to Apollonius, a festival was held here in his day, at which the island women would josh the men, re-enacting what happened when the Argonauts, with no oil for the alter in their shrine, used water from the spring as their offering. For this they were mocked by Medea – the princess and priestess of Colchis, who had helped Jason to find the Fleece – and her women, who had come back to Greece with him. The custom disappeared when the Roman world, including Greece, turned Christian in the late fifth century AD. The temple was closed, and in the next recording of the shrine its patron is no longer the 'great healer', but the 'life-giving source', the freshwater spring by the ruins of the ancient temple.

For the searcher after myths the legend of Anafe is both an incentive and a warning. It suggests the longevity of myth and the seductive possibilities of continuity; but it warns of the danger of assuming it. The history of the temple site was a blank for over a thousand years up to the seventeenth century, and like many of the small Cyclades, Anafe was depopulated in the Middle Ages. So there was no certainty that any of the population would hang on to pass down the traditions of this sacred place. Nonetheless the tale is testimony to the popularity of the Argonaut legend, which spread all round the shores of the Mediterranean and the Black Sea in classical times.

The story of the Golden Fleece is between three and four millennia old, going back into the deepest layers of Greek culture. Endlessly retold and reinterpreted, it is one of the oldest tales of the hero's quest: a journey to a sinister El Dorado, the first mysterious land to draw adventurers across the seas in search of fortune and everlasting fame.

Previous pages: *The Golden Fleece* by Herbert Draper (1904). The story of Jason and the Argonauts is often reduced to a Boys Own version of the hero's quest. But it is a very dark tale: here, having taken the Fleece, Jason's lover Medea prepares to kill and dismember her own brother to distract their pursuers.

THE ROOTS OF GREEK MYTH

The Greeks are perhaps the greatest myth-makers in history: Apollo and Dionysos, Aphrodite and Artemis, Minos and the Minotaur, Oedipus, the legends of Thebes and Troy, still captivate the world today. These myths and stories are the roots of classical Greek religion and culture, and most go back to the Bronze Age, in the second millennium BC. They continue to move us because they deal in unchanging human verities – love and hatred, courage, loyalty and the terrible power of the irrational. Modern psychologists see them as archetypal because they seem to draw on the deep past of the human psyche and, after all, the world we live in is still shaken by events of atavistic cruelty, despite our much vaunted modernity. Greek myths expose this dark undercurrent and articulate better, perhaps, than any other literature, the battle between the noble and the base in the human psyche. They illustrate the soul's conflict with evil, which is one of the central concerns of the myths of the world, from the Sumerian *Epic of Gilgamesh* to *Star Wars* and *The Lord of the Rings*.

The tale of Jason is set in the generation before the Trojan War, let's say before 1300 BC, but we first find it mentioned six centuries later in the age of Homer. Composing perhaps not long before 700 BC, the author of the *Odyssey* says that the story of the *Argo* was by then well known to everybody. The sorceress Circe tells Odysseus on his wanderings about the legendary ship the *Argo* in her account of the Wandering Rocks:

> The only sea voyaging ship to have sailed there is *Argo* – a story
> which everyone knows – on her voyage from Aietes. She too would
> have shattered on the great rocks but Hera escorted her through,
> since Jason was dear to her.

Homer mentions other parts of the story which were also common knowledge in his time: Circe, for example, is said to be the sister of 'savage-minded Aietes', the king who lived in the extreme east, in a land called Aia – the land of the Golden

Overleaf: Jason's outward voyage to Colchis, modern Georgia. It is possible that a Bronze Age journey into the Black Sea underlies the story, but we should not forget the element of fantasy: the return journeys (inset) reflect different stages in the growth of the Greeks' geographical knowledge, which were incorporated into fiction.

Jason's outward journey

0　　　　　　150 km

Jason's return journeys
version in Hesiod, eighth century BC
Apollonius's version, third century BC
Egyptian version, approx. AD 500
(but possibly pre-Hesiod)

Danube

Cape Acheron
(Cave of Hades)

'Clashing Rocks'

Istanbul

Sea of
Marmara

Samothrace

Erdek

Volos

Lemnos　　Troy

Aegean
Sea

GREECE

TURKEY

Anafe

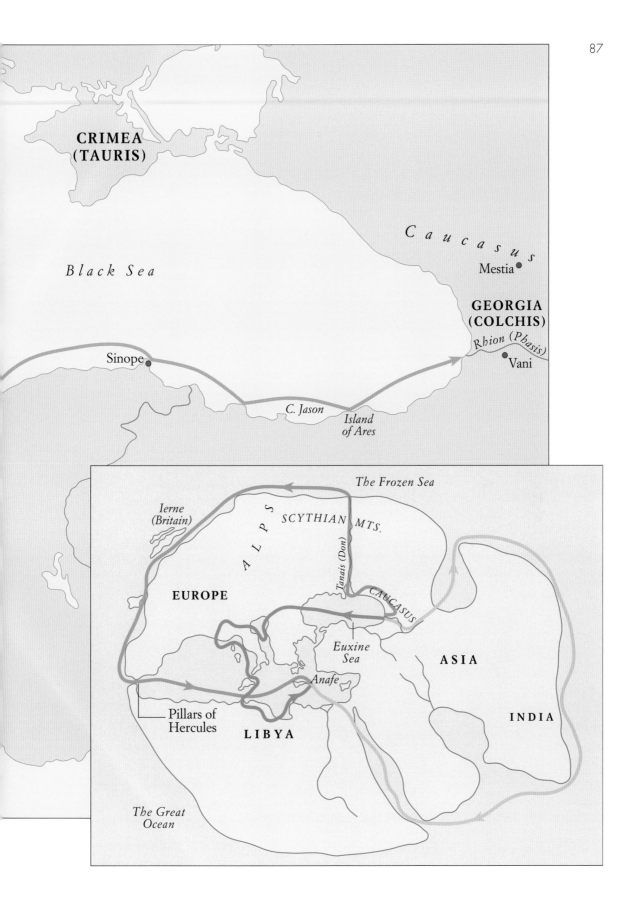

**CRIMEA
(TAURIS)**

Black Sea

C a u c a s u s

Mestia

**GEORGIA
(COLCHIS)**

Rhion (Phasis)

Vani

Sinope

C. Jason

*Island
of Ares*

The Frozen Sea

*Ierne
(Britain)*

A L P S SCYTHIAN MTS.

Tanais (Don)

C A U C A S U S

EUROPE

*Euxine
Sea*

ASIA

Pillars of
Hercules

Anafe

LIBYA

INDIA

*The Great
Ocean*

Fleece. Homer also knows of Aietes' daughter Medea, the divine priestess who helps Jason fulfil his task and becomes his lover, wife and eventual nemesis. From this one might guess that even before Homer there were narrative poems which told the tale of the heroic voyage to the fairyland of Aia.

After Homer there are many retellings of the tale in literature and in art. In the eighth century BC the Boeotian poet Hesiod mentions Pelias, King of Iolkos, who in some versions unjustly took the throne of Jason's father. It was Pelias, 'over-proud, violent and outrageous, a doer of savage deeds', who imposed on Jason the task of gaining the Fleece. Hesiod is the first to mention the river Phasis as the goal of Jason's expedition, though where it was he does not say. Hesiod also says that on their return the Argonauts sailed from the mouth of the Phasis into the Great Ocean, circled the world to Libya (Africa) and brought the *Argo* back to Greece from the south. Perhaps it was this older version of the tale that gave rise to the Anafe legend. At any rate, when we first pick it up in the eighth century BC this was a fairy-tale voyage, just like Odysseus's, not a journey to be placed on any literal map.

Not long after 700 BC, the poet Eumelos was the first to place the kingdom of Aia, the land of the sun where the Fleece was kept. This was in Colchis, beside the river Phasis, in today's Georgia, which at that time was held to mark the eastern edge of the known world. From this point on (though not necessarily before), we can be sure that the legend describes an expedition to the Black Sea. For a first complete version we have to wait till the fifth century BC, when the lyric poet Pindar names some of the Greek heroes who went with Jason, including for the first time Heracles (Hercules). Pindar lived during the Persian wars, when the Greeks defeated the almost overwhelming power of a great Asiatic empire. At this time they began to define themselves against the exotic and savage Other, 'inventing the barbarian', as it were, and the Argonaut legend was now reshaped as a clash of civilizations. Already a savage land of strange customs, the fairyland of Aia was depicted as a malevolent and alien world, where the norms of Greek culture were turned upside down. This tale was told by the great tragic dramatists of the fifth century BC, when Medea takes centre stage. Princess and priestess, granddaughter of the Sun God, the dark and fascinating heroine of the story was now the key dramatic figure. Breaking with her land, people, father and kin, she butchers her own brother, and, eventually, in the most terrifying breach of norms, even kills her own children.

The journey of the *Argo* reached what is essentially its final version in the third century BC, in the period after Alexander the Great's invasion of Asia. Its author, Apollonius of Rhodes, was head of the great library in Alexandria. By his time Greek geographical knowledge had advanced considerably, and old perceptions had to be fitted to a new world. The archaic idea that the Argonauts sailed out of the river Phasis into the Great Ocean and came back via Africa was now out of date. Apollonius offers us instead an elaborate geographical fantasy in which the Argonauts escape from the Black Sea up the Danube, cross overland into the Adriatic and then wander round the eastern Mediterranean, much as Odysseus does in the *Odyssey*. Apollonius had access to every kind of learning, and he mixes fairy-tale with accurate topographical detail and both real and fabulous ethnography in a manner that recalls modern novelists such as Philip Pullman in his *Dark Materials* trilogy. Arrow-shooting birds, Amazons and Sirens rub shoulders with realistically grimy ironworkers and silver miners on the Black Sea coast; the Argonauts visit the wooden pillar houses of the Pontic Alps, and observe the weird funeral customs of the Colchians who wrap male corpses in hides and hang them in trees. All this was part of the great pool of new knowledge of the world in the Hellenistic Greek age after Alexander the Great.

Apollonius's version is the best-known one, the one which has come down to us in paintings, novels, plays, operas and Hollywood films. But there are Roman versions by Valerius Flaccus, Seneca and Ovid (used by Shakespeare). There are medieval romances, in which Jason is a Christian knight; Renaissance books and plays; and the tale is popular in Romantic and Pre-Raphaelite art. In the twentieth century there have been memorable cinematic versions including those by Pasolini (starring Maria Callas) and Lars von Trier. In recent years the figure of Medea has inspired fascinating feminist readings. Ever since the time of Homer, in fact, and for probably long before that, the tale has been retold and reshaped, and it still has the power to speak to us today. But what lies behind the myth? Was there, for example, a real journey? Who was Jason? And what is the meaning of the Golden Fleece?

THE START OF THE QUEST

> What was the beginning of their voyage? And what danger held
> them in strong adamantine bolts? It was appointed that Pelias must
> die by the hands of Aiolos's proud sons … A prophecy came to him,
> chilling his weary heart. Spoken at the midmost navel-stone of earth,
> fair-forested mother: 'Let him beware at all costs. The man with one
> sandal. When he comes from the homesteads in the hills to the sunny
> plains of great Iolkos.'
> PINDAR *Fourth Pythian Ode* 463 BC

Deprived of his parents and his rightful inheritance, the throne of Iolkos, Jason is brought up on Mount Pelion in Thessaly by the kindly centaur Cheiron. His wicked uncle King Pelias (think *Hamlet* or *The Lion King*) has usurped his father's throne but lives under the shadow of the oracle's prophecy that he must fear the *monosandalos*: the man with one shoe. Aged twenty, clad in animal skin, with long hair, a young warrior who is parentless and uninitiated, Jason comes down to his ancestral town and loses a sandal in the river Anaurus while carrying across a toothless old crone who has asked for his help. This turns out to be Hera, queen of the gods, who will be his protectress. (Jason charms all the women, although perhaps he loves no one but himself.) In Iolkos, Jason comes before King Pelias, reveals who he is and claims his kingdom. The king says: 'If I am to give you the kingdom, first *you must bring me the Golden Fleece.*'

So, a fairy-tale beginning. The hero is set his quest: to go beyond the edge of the known world on a kind of Mission Impossible. But what *was* the Golden Fleece? This is where the tale of Phrixus comes in. An ancestor of Jason, Phrixus had long ago flown from Greece on the back of a magical golden ram, belonging to Zeus, King of the Gods, himself. Phrixus had flown east to the land of Colchis, whose king, Aietes, was the son of Helios, the Sun God. Aietes sacrifices the ram and hangs its fleece in a sacred grove guarded by a fearsome dragon. (An oracle foretold that Aietes too would lose his kingdom if he lost the Fleece.) But why a fleece, and why was it thought to have such a supernatural aura?

Fleeces are connected with magic in many folk traditions. Even now in rural Greece you can find the custom of wrapping the sick in a freshly killed fleece. But in the ancient world it was a much more potent symbol. In the prophetic books of the ancient Etruscans, for example, a gold-coloured fleece was a prophecy of future prosperity for clan and kingdom. This perhaps fits with the idea in some versions of the tale that Jason must possess the Fleece before he can become King of Iolkos; similarly King Aietes will forfeit the throne of Colchis if he gives it up. Recent discoveries from the Hittite empire in late Bronze Age Anatolia have cast new light on all this. At the New Year festival, consecrated rams' fleeces were hung on tree totems in temples as part of the rituals in which royal power was renewed each spring. As we shall see, these rituals also included a kind of sacred recital through which a hero killed a dragon with the help of a divine female helper.

These tantalizing hints may offer us clues to the form and meaning of the earliest layers of the myth. To search for the Fleece was to search for a divine talisman, which was also an auspicious and magical symbol of kingship. Jason's quest was for fame and glory, but also to regain his father's kingdom.

THE LAND OF JASON AND THE HEROIC AGE

Since the 1870s, a sensational series of excavations at Mycenae, Tiryns, Knossos, Troy, Pylos and elsewhere have brought to life the Heroic Age. They have also proved that the Greek myths and the epic poems of Homer and his successors have preserved genuine traditions of Bronze Age society, and even perhaps of real events such as the siege of Troy. We now know that Jason's city of Iolkos was the centre of a real Bronze Age Greek kingdom. Its modern successor is the city of Volos, which nestles below the green flanks of Mount Pelion on a magnificent bay in one of the most beautiful parts of Greece. It was always a seafaring place and Volos is still a thriving port today. Around the Gulf of Volos archaeologists have identified many sites from the Heroic Age, and recent excavations have dramatically added colour to the legend. In 1997 a late Bronze Age palace was uncovered a couple of kilometres inland on the coastal plain close by the important prehistoric site of Dimini. Spectacular finds so far include a royal *megaron*, or reception hall, with an intact hearth altar for sacrifices, and heaps of pottery lying where they fell when the palace was destroyed. Though some way from the sea in the late Bronze Age, the palace was reachable by boat up a long inlet – in ancient Greek an *ialka*, which is perhaps where the name Iolkos came from. Here, if anywhere, more clues to Jason's ancestral home will be found – possibly even written texts on clay tablets.

What is also worth bearing in mind when we consider the genesis of the Argonaut legend is that this area of Thessaly is now known to have been a centre of the development of early epic poetry in the centuries before Homer. Indeed it was perhaps in palaces like Iolkos in the late Bronze Age that Greek bards first advanced from heroic songs or praise poems of a few hundred lines to extended epics of several thousand, telling stories of many episodes. There are parallels, for example, between the Troy story and the Jason saga, both stories of an expedition by sea to a land in the east by a company of heroes who go through tremendous struggles to reach their goal. And whatever the later mythic overlay, if the Troy epic was based on real events, as it now seems, so might also be the tale of the Argonauts.

THE CAVE OF CHEIRON THE CENTAUR

In the legend Jason was brought up by the centaur Cheiron in the forests of Mount Pelion. Half man, half horse, the wise Cheiron was the tutor not only of Jason, but of the hero Achilles and Asklepios, the founder of medicine. Today you can go up Pelion from Volos on a delightful railway that runs along the shore and then climbs up into the wooded mountains overlooking the bay. The train stops at the little station of Milies, deep in the forest, and from there one walks up to the summit through shadowy glades of huge and ancient trees. It's easy to imagine that this was once a dwelling place of demi-gods and spirits. On top of Pelion, nearly a century ago, the remains were discovered of a shrine to the king of the gods, Zeus Akraios, 'Zeus of the heights'. Among the trees the excavators also found a collapsed cave, the cave where legend said Cheiron had lived. In and around the cave were found votive offerings to Cheiron 'the healer', left by pilgrims. In ancient times strange legends were told of this place with dark suggestions of human sacrifice. A Hellenistic writer tells how the locals went up to the cave, sacrificed rams and dressed up in the freshly flayed skins:

> On the heights of Mount Pelion, there is a cave, the so-called cave
> of Cheiron, and a shrine of Zeus Akraios. At Sirius's rising, which is
> the time of the greatest heat, the most prominent citizens, those in
> the prime of their lives, climb up into the cave. They are chosen by
> the priest and girded with fresh, thrice-shorn sheepskins.

Something uncannily like this ritual seems to have taken place here even in the last century. Every May Day a procession went up to the summit, where an old man in a black sheepskin mask and costume was ritually 'killed' and brought back to life by his companions, dressed in white fleeces. In ancient times the ceremony was performed by the rulers of the Pelion region in the name of 'Zeus of the mountain top'. This gives us another clue to the deeper layers of the myth of the Golden Fleece: to the fleece as an emblem of auspiciousness, rooted in the sacrificial rituals of the Bronze Age.

When you come down from the mountain and head on foot round the bay towards the palace at Dimini, you go through olive groves, and past smallholdings and allotments till you come to the dried-up bed of the river Xerias. This was the river Anaurus, where Jason carried Hera, queen of the gods, on his way to claim his inheritance. Turn downriver towards the sea, and in half an hour or so you reach Pagasae, the old port of Iolkos. The ruined fortifications and towers in the fields are from the period after Alexander the Great, but Pagasae has been inhabited continuously since prehistory. There was a famous oracle here, an altar to Apollo, and it was here, according to legend, that Jason's ship the *Argo* ('Swift') was built.

Jutting into the glassy waters of the bay is a wooded promontory, with a solitary palm tree and little shrine to the Apostles. At its foot is a creek with a careening yard where yachts are pulled up on the shingle; nearby two rusting

Above: A modern reconstruction of the *Argo*, based on depictions of Iron Age boats. Into the beech keel is set the upright stem of oak, which, in the myth, came from the whispering oak at the oracle of Dodona.

steamers lie grounded in the shallows among the rotting skeletons of old wooden boats. Across the inlet is a traditional shipbuilding yard, where fishing caiques are built of Pelion pine, just like the *Argo*. Here the master builder is building a new *Argo*, modelled on early images of Aegean boats including a graffito of an eighth-century BC oared boat from Volos. He is experimenting with the old techniques: 30 metres long, the keel is simply three huge beech trees pegged together with long oak pins, then soaked with water and bent with ropes and chains to pull the stern into a long tapering curve. The vessel has no frame; the twenty-five rowing benches will hold the hull in shape. In the prow a massive 3-metre upright forms the stern where the speaking oak from the oracle at Dodona was placed in the legend. So seemingly primitive, the three tree trunks look like a giant bow 30 metres long. 'The hardest thing,' says the master builder, 'is to think like them. To think simply.' Standing by it, you imagine, surely it was something like this.

Outside the sun is setting golden over the still-blue bay. The shipyard hands and old salts sit smoking roll-ups on the shore by the hulk of the steamer *Maria*, which once plied her trade to the Black Sea and the Levant. A fitting place for the great adventure to begin.

THE CREW

> Now I shall recount the lineage and names of the heroes, their voyages over the vast sea, and all they achieved on their wanderings …'
> APOLLONIUS OF RHODES *The Voyage of Argo c.* 250 BC

In the final version of the tale all the most famous Greek heroes are recruited for the voyage, including Heracles (Hercules) himself. This is how it is told in all the modern screen versions. But fragments of earlier poems show that originally the crew were Minyans, men of Thessaly. Of that original mythic crew only a few names survive, among them the seers Idmon and Mopsus and the helmsman Tiphys, all of whom die on the voyage. In later days all the towns of Greece vied with each other to have a hero on the great voyage, swelling the crew list from the original fifty to over a hundred. Later additions to the cast of characters include Asklepios as the ship's doctor, and the musician Orpheus (who is depicted with the *Argo* in a sixth-century BC sculpture at Delphi). Heracles himself first appears in the fifth century BC and was probably not part of the original myth. As for Jason himself, intriguingly his name appears to be recorded on Bronze Age tablets as *I-wa-son*: a name that may mean 'the healer'. Could this be a hint of his mythic role in earlier versions of the tale?

THE ARGO SETS SAIL: THE JOURNEY TO LEMNOS

So the Argo set sail from the lovely promontory of Pagasae, in its prow the speaking beam cut from the whispering oak tree at the oracle in 'wintry' Dodona. In the many tellings of the myth the *Argo* is often said to be the first boat, but perhaps this means the first ocean-going boat. After all, people had sailed the Aegean since before 5000 BC, trading metals and obsidian. And beautiful murals from Thera, from the seventeenth century BC, show elegant boats at festival time with long curved prows, propelled by both sails and oars. Greece has been a bridge between continents since prehistory, and as any traveller knows it is possible to sail from the mainland to Asia – island hopping, hugging the peninsulas and promontories – without ever losing sight of land. As Plato put it, Mediterranean people live 'like frogs around a frog pond' and in the sailing season these were not journeys to inspire fear. As we know, however, the *Argo's* quest was to go beyond the familiar, into the unknown.

Above: Anchoring overnight off the coast of Magnesia on the way to Lemnos. A fifty-oared Bronze or Iron Age boat would have been about 25 metres long. Overleaf: The old Turkish harbour at Lemnos today, with the castle beyond.

The Argonauts' first stop was Lemnos: a rugged hilly island 100 kilometres or so out in the northeast Aegean, and the main stepping stone on the way to the Dardanelles and the Black Sea. (The British used its great natural harbour in Moudros Bay as their naval base in the Gallipoli campaign.) In Greek myth Lemnos was the island of the smith god Hephaestus and was long known for its metalworking: Homer calls the island 'smoke shrouded'.

Lemnos has known many waves of invaders, of whom the Greeks were by no means the first. Above the main port at Myrina, brooding volcanic crags are topped by a dramatic castle built in turn by Byzantines, Venetians, Genoese and Turks. In the old 'Turkish harbour' an Ottoman house bears the date of the Muslim calendar; by the big *kafeneion* where the fishermen take their ouzo and coffee, a fountain with an Arabic inscription still flows; the gateway to the madrasa garden now frames the door to the supermarket which masks a fine octagonal Turkish bath.

The story of the Argonauts' stay at Lemnos is a very strange one. The heroes go ashore and find an alien place inhabited only by women who have murdered their men as a result of a curse laid on the Lemnians by Aphrodite, goddess of love, for impugning her virtue. The women were cursed with a disgusting smell which repelled their husbands. (The smell, incidentally, has been explained by the old island tradition of dyeing cloth with murex shells – a particularly foul-smelling job which was carried on in Bronze Age Lemnos.) When their men took new wives from Thrace, the women got them drunk and threw them off a cliff, which local legend still points out at Petassos. It's a tale that is typical of a number of Greek myths where powerful independent women are seen as threatening to the patriarchal order, and demonized as sinister breakers of norms. The Argonauts, of course, know nothing of the Lemnians' dark secret and find themselves on a fairy island of women who, unusually in a traditional heroic society, are free, sexually active and itching to take them to bed. Confronted by a boatload of handsome and vigorous heroes, the women spruce themselves up and set about enthusiastically repopulating the island. A generation later, when the Greeks land here on their way to Troy, they are victualled by Jason's son by Queen Hypsipyle.

Of course, this all sounds like pure fairy story, but the tale was already known to Homer which suggests that it is a very early part of the legend. As Homer knew, Lemnos was not Greek in the Heroic Age; its language is still undeciphered but has

Opposite, top: The Neolithic and Bronze Age town of 'smoky Lemnos' was at Poliochni on a wide bay facing the coast of Anatolia and the Dardanelles.
Opposite, below: Grand stone buildings suggest the wealth of Lemnos.

no known relation to Greek; and its burial customs mysteriously seem to have affinities with the ancient Etruscans, who are believed to have migrated to Italy from the Aegean. Recent archaeological evidence shows that the island had the most advanced Neolithic civilization in the Aegean, going back to around 4000 BC. Its biggest centre was the large Bronze Age town at Poliochni, which is presumably the 'Lemnos' of the Argonaut myth. Defended by massive prehistoric fortifications, Poliochni stands on a high bluff above a wide bay where long rollers crash on to the island's eastern shore, driven by the powerful currents that rush down from the Dardanelles. Recent discoveries here suggest no contact with the Greek world until the middle Bronze Age, around 1400 BC, when pottery was imported from the region of Iolkos, of all places. With their alien language, the people here remained virtual strangers to the Greeks until colonized towards 700 BC, by which time the Lemnian episode was already fixed in the Argonaut legend. And a last tantalizing clue is the most recent of all: analysis of the metal ores smelted on the island as far back as the early Bronze Age shows they came to Lemnos from the Black Sea coast en route to Colchis. If the Lemnians had long known the metal-bearing regions of the Black Sea, then maybe the Greeks did too?

THE ISLAND OF THE GREAT GODS

On a clear day the great bulk of the island of Samothrace, with its jagged peaks and ravines, rears up beyond the northern shore of Lemnos. Rugged and magical, Samothrace is an island of forests, waterfalls and pools, with glades of ancient plane trees – a real abode of the gods. This is where the legend says the Argonauts sailed next, to be initiated into the mysterious cult of the Kabeiroi, the 'Great Gods'. This strange cult with its non-Greek gods and its pre-Greek language gave special protection to seafarers, but whether this episode has any authority earlier than the third century BC, when Apollonius included it in his version, is not known.

From Samothrace they pass Troy by night (the tale is set in the era before the Trojan War when Troy still controlled the Dardanelles) and then enter the Sea of Marmara where islands seem to float on the calm summer waters of what was a Greek sea for two millennia. A founding myth for the towns along its shore, the tale of Jason was long remembered here, and the sites of individual episodes have

Opposite: Samothrace – the Sanctuary of the Great Gods. The Argonauts' initiation here was probably an invention of Apollonius in the third century BC, based on a much older story of their visit to the shrine of the Kabeiroi on Lemnos.

been identified from ancient times right up to the early twentieth century. For example, on the peninsula of Artaki, today's Erdek, the local King of Cyzikus entertains the Argonauts hospitably but is then killed accidentally in a confused night-time skirmish after the *Argo* is driven back in a storm. To beg the gods' forgiveness and to expiate the sin of blood guilt, Jason climbs Mount Didymos (the 'twins'), the double-peaked mountain on the peninsula which was still known as Didymos by local Greeks into the twentieth century. On its summit Jason offers sacrifices to the great goddess of the land, Cybele, and the ship's carpenter makes a wooden statue of her for a little shrine there, the remains of which were still visible at the start of the twentieth century.

The Argonauts sail on, coasting the lovely shore of Marmara. At this point Heracles jumps ship in grief after he loses his beautiful page, Hylas. (As with Achilles and Patroclus one should never underestimate the heroes' love for boys in these myths!) The site where Hylas vanished was also later made into a shrine, and strangely enough it is still an Islamic place of pilgrimage today. Of course, we need take none of these stories literally as records of a real journey done at the end of the Bronze Age. The Sea of Marmara was not colonized by the Greeks till the eighth century BC, and fascinating as they are, these local shrines and stories are testimonies to the myth, not to history.

INTO THE BOSPHORUS

We are leaving Istanbul, the former Constantinople, heading for the Bosphorus. Originally a Megaran colony called Byzantion, for nearly three millennia the city has been the gateway to the Black Sea and the northern world, which the legend says was opened up by Jason and the Argonauts.

Inside the 30 kilometres of the Bosphorus the current sweeps down from the north, creating alarming eddies and currents around the bays and headlands. No wonder that to Greek eyes getting through to the Black Sea was such a mythic feat. Several legends are told of the Argonauts' journey here: the defeat of the bullying local chief Amycus; the deliverance of the blind prophet Phineus from the Harpies, the filthy winged monsters who kept him in perpetual torment; and Phineus's prophecy to Jason which told him how to be the first mariner ever to sail through the 'Clashing Rocks' and enter the ocean beyond.

Opposite: Istanbul straddles two worlds: the great Byzantine monuments and Ottoman mosques stand on the site of a Greek colony of c. 700 BC.

A fascinating Christianized version of the Amycus tale is told by John Malalas in the sixth century AD: when the Argonauts were attacked by Amycus's forces they sought refuge in a secluded cove, where they had a vision of a man with wings like an eagle. The figure prophesied their victory over Amycus, and the grateful Argonauts built a temple in which they set up a statue of the apparition. They called the site 'Sosthenion' because they had been saved there. According to the legend, when the first Christian Roman emperor, Constantine, visited the temple he recognized the statue as 'an angel in the habit of a monk'. The identity of the angel as St Michael was revealed to him in a dream, and Constantine built the Michaelion in honour of the archangel. The site became famous for miraculous healings and even apparitions of the archangel. Visited by the emperor Anastasius in AD 511, it was for a long time a place of pilgrimage until it vanished from the record in the fourteenth century when the Turks overran western Anatolia.

Today the spot is marked by the little port and repair yard of Istinye (whose name comes from the Greek *stenion*). It is a secluded bay tucked into the wooded slopes of the Bosphorus, its quay lined with electronics shops, fish restaurants and yacht chandlers. I asked our captain whether there was still a pilgrimage place in Istinye today, expecting a Muslim mosque, and he directed me up a lane between shops, and up a flight of steps to a gate topped with a Byzantine cross. Inside was a little garden, with pink and lilac hydrangeas in pots, and a fine old Orthodox church, its walls built out of reused ancient stonework, and with the remains of classical marble, including a fine libation tray, littered about the yard. The church was locked, and a Turkish lady leaned out of a nearby window and told me the *pappas* was away till Saturday. But through the vestibule windows I could see a tray with a coffee pot, a Turkish newspaper, and on the wall an icon of St Michael. So this was the famous medieval pilgrimage place of the archangel, which still marks the site of a much more ancient pagan shrine commemorating the Argonauts.

That afternoon we pushed on between the great forts of Sultan Mehmet II at the narrows – the 'Devil's Rocks' to local seamen – and on to the mouth of the Black Sea, where Greek tradition located the famous 'Clashing Rocks' mentioned in both the Argonaut legend and the *Odyssey*. There have been many theories (Robert Graves thought they were great sheets of ice washed down from the Crimea!), but when you sail through them in a small boat the myth instantly makes sense. The rocks stand petrified in an 'open' position at the northern end of the Bosphorus, jagged teeth battered by the northerlies that sweep in down the Bulgarian coast. It is easy to see how the first sailors to get through them might have told stories about such a landmark. Not so much about getting through to the

Black Sea, though that is still a feat of seamanship in a sailing boat, as getting back. No doubt the myth arose with the Greek penetration of the Black Sea, when brave sea captains negotiated these perilous waters for the first time. From then on the founding of colonies on the sea's shore and the mastery of its currents turned it in Greek eyes from the Axeinos Pontus, the 'Hostile Sea', to the Euxeinos Pontus, the 'Welcoming Sea'.

THE GREEKS IN THE BLACK SEA

Once the jagged rocks are behind you, the sea opens out. This is what the Greeks called the Pontus, 'the Sea'. Its vast basin measures over 1 million square kilometres, while the sea itself is less than a fifth of that. It is swelled by forty rivers, some small, some great – the Danube, Bug Dnieper, Dniester and Don – their combined waters pouring down to the Bosphorus. With only the one narrow outlet, no wonder it is so dangerous to enter the strait from the north. A shipping guide from the end of the age of sail mentions four hundred wrecks in one thirty-year period in the late nineteenth century. However, sailing on the sea itself is 'neither difficult nor dangerous', as the 1850s *Black Sea Pilot* says reassuringly. On the outward journey, once you are through the rocks and turn eastwards towards the rising sun, the circular current of the sea bears you along the Turkish coast all the way to Georgia. And so it did the Argonauts and all who came afterwards in the centuries when the Euxine was a Greek sea.

The Greek adventure in the Black Sea lasted three thousand years, a colonization for which at that point there was no precursor in history. And, amazingly, Greeks are still there along the Bulgarian and Romanian coast. Take today's Sozpol, the ancient Apollonia, founded around 600 BC, and still a Greek-speaking town today. Further north there is the lonely island of Fido Nisi at the mouth of the Danube, where legend has it the spirit of Achilles was flown after his death before the walls of Troy. The Black Sea world is stuffed with Greek myth as far as the Crimea and the Sea of Azov – the region of ancient Tauris, where Iphigenia lived in exile and Heracles performed his tenth labour.

Tempting as it is to seek some historical core to the myths, they obviously only became attached to these remote places when the Greeks had been there. And when the Greeks arrived there is controversial. The first colonies date from around 700 BC, maybe a little before. At that time Homer knew several place names along the southern Black Sea coast, but of the lands east of Sinope he knew nothing, and maybe this represents the extent of knowledge in his day. But this doesn't tell us when the Greeks first explored or raided this coast. Did they even get through into the Black Sea in the Bronze Age, as the legend suggests? Fascinatingly, this is still an open question. There is evidence on the Romanian coast in the form of anchors, ingots and pottery, and many are prepared to believe that they really got there then; that the Jason tale is ultimately based on a real adventure before the dawn of Greek history.

As we have seen, the myth is set in the Heroic Age before the Trojan War, around 1300 BC, if not well back into the fourteenth century. But all myths gather detail and change over time. Suppose there was an early poem about a real chieftain of Iolkos who went on a daring journey to a faraway magic land to get some kind of magical treasure. Perhaps this was the version 'on everyone's lips' in Homer's time. Now it is just possible that this hypothetical tale had the hero passing beyond the 'Clashing Rocks' into the Great Ocean, which in early Greek belief surrounded the earth. Only later perhaps does the tale get fixed in Colchis, when the Greeks were founding their first colonies on the Pontic coast. It is, I guess, just possible that Bronze Age Greeks had heard of Colchis through Anatolian intermediaries, but more likely the heroic journey into the unknown became located in the Caucasus only after the Greeks had got there. Whichever way it started, in time the tale became not only a rattling good story, but also a colonization myth: 'The Argonauts were there before us.' Thereafter, every little place from Sicily to the Sea of Azov (and even little Anafe!) claimed its own piece of the Argonaut legend. Long before it became a novel in the hands of Apollonius, the story had become the founding myth of the Black Sea Greeks.

SAILING TO TREBIZOND

So our journey pushed on, with Apollonius in hand, from the Bosphorus along the Black Sea coast to Georgia. We moved eastwards, partly by road, partly coasting with local captains and fishermen. East of Sinope the coast had no roads till very recently, and snow-capped mountain ranges come right down to the water's edge. The only connections that could be made in the old days were by sea. Almost into our own time shipping companies connected Trebizond, Sinope, the smaller ports and the coaling stations such as Zonguldak, ancient Heracleia. Even up to the Second World War these were run by Greek businessmen of the quaintly named Société Ottomane d'Héraclée, proud of their 2600-year-old traditions.

We sailed past towns whose names barely conceal their Greek origins – Eregli (another Heracleia) and Tiribolu (Tripolis) – where crumbling Byzantine castles jut

Above: Soumela monastery in the Pontic Alps near Trabzon (Trebizond). The Greeks left their mark on the landscape of the Black Sea coast from ancient times until their expulsion in 1922.

over the surf on fairy-tale crags. Lovely wooded valleys spread down from the Pontic Alps and streams pour ice-blue over pebbly beds as they rush across the narrow plain. Centuries ago these little places too were only reachable by boat: no road led from the interior of Anatolia. This coast was entirely opened up by seafaring, and in a real sense Jason's journey is a metaphor for this.

It was on a beautiful summer's evening that we rounded Yason Burnu, the ancient Cape Jason, looking for a sandy shore to make camp for the night. Here we came upon what I called the 'iron beach': a thick black bank on the shore which left great hairy clumps on my magnet. In the Jason myth there is a tale of a land of iron on this same bit of coast, with a population of ironworkers who toil in grime and smoke and blackness. The same tale is mentioned in the eighth century BC by Homer; much later Marco Polo tells of the iron and silver mines around Argyropolis, 'Silver Town'; and even into the twentieth century the Greeks monopolized ironworking, sending miners as far as Cappodocia and the Euphrates, in Syria and Mesopotamia, zealously guarding the craft for the Greek

Above: The blacksmith in Tonya. This region has long been known for its metalworking, a craft whose roots go back to the Bronze Age or even earlier. Ores smelted on Neolithic Lemnos came from this part of the Pontic coast.

community. In a village up a country lane inland from the coast, the present-day blacksmith in his forge told me how his father had been a blacksmith too, but in those days only Greeks had the 'mystery' and would not pass it on to a Muslim. So his father had to go elsewhere to learn his trade.

THE PONTIC GREEKS

In the valleys running down to the Black Sea shore around Trebizond, the Greek presence lasted from 700 BC until our own time. Only after the catastrophe of 1922, when the Greeks were expelled from Turkey, did most of them migrate to Greece, or into Georgia where many had started to go before the First World War when the first signs of burning were in the air. The Turks had entered central Anatolia (the Greek word for 'the east') in the eleventh century, and by 1400 it was entirely in their hands, though the jewel in the crown, Constantinople itself, wasn't taken till 1453. By then the Greek-speaking Christian population was in a minority, and even their church services were conducted partly in Greek, partly in Turkish.

In Pontus, on the Black Sea coast, it was a different story. Here the Greeks were a very strong presence right up into modern times. Although they had been conquered in 1486, they were still the majority in the seventeenth century and many who converted to Islam still spoke Greek. Even in the late twentieth century the authorities in Trebizond had to use interpreters to work with the Muslim Pontic-Greek speakers in the law courts, as the language was still spoken as their mother tongue. This region had a thriving oral culture into the last century and a whole genre of ballads comes down from the ancient Greeks: tales of supernatural intervention in which ordinary objects have a mystic symbolism. Birds talk and take messages, the dead go not to the Christian heaven or hell but to a grim underworld ruled by Kharos, the ancient Charon, who ferried souls across the river Styx. You could even hear the Cyclops story from the tale-tellers of Pontus, only it is not Odysseus's men that he seizes but seven Orthodox priests, one of whom he proceeds to roast and eat! (The rest, though, still escape in a truly Homeric way, heating a spit which they drive into Cyclops's eye before fleeing his cave dressed in sheepskins.)

Hoping to find surviving speakers of 'Rumja' or 'Romaika' – Pontic Greek – we pushed into the interior, to the villages around Tonya on a day when clouds sat heavily on the dark-green mountain slopes amid intermittent squalls of rain. Although it was July, the air was dank and chill and we gratefully drank hot soup

in the café. Then, sitting under the trees in the square, where the old men drink thick sweet Turkish coffee, we listened as they started telling tales. We heard Greek words; then the younger men joined in, and it was a real surprise to find their generation bilingual, as it is said to be among the older women that the language has survived best.

With rain now dripping off the awnings of the café, someone arrived with an old three-stringed lyre, the traditional instrument of the Pontic Greeks, and as the lamps came on, amid distant muffled rolls of thunder, the old folks began dancing the ancient rounds. They call it the *horon* in Turkish, but this is actually the Greek word for the dance. We quaffed our coffees and rakis and joined in. That afternoon, as we danced in the square, I had an intimation that we were watching the last act of the story that had begun with Jason's mythical voyage; but, as we were to discover in Georgia, that time has not quite come yet.

Above: Story-tellers in Tonya. Turkish Sunni Muslims, they also speak the old Pontic dialect of Greek and are living witnesses to the extraordinary richness of the history of Anatolia.
Opposite: The traditional three-stringed lyre is still played on the Black Sea coast of Turkey.

THE ISLAND OF ARES AND THE BLACK STONE

The next day we sailed on from Giresun (the classical Greek Gerasounda) past the ancient Cape Zephyros. Ahead of us we soon made out one of the rare islands on this coast, small and steep, with decaying medieval fortifications towering over the seaward side amid dense woods. As we moved in closer, thousands of birds rose from the trees and circled around. In the myth this was the Island of Ares, the god of war, where clouds of frightening birds showered the Argonauts with dart-like feathers resembling porcupine quills. Having driven them off (by banging their weapons on their shields) the Argonauts landed and sacrificed at a black stone altar which had been set up by the Amazon queen Antiope, who lived on the coast opposite. These days, after some remarkable finds in the steppes of central Asia, scholars are more prepared to believe in societies of female warriors than they once were, but as yet not here. The shrine on the island, however, was real; it was later the site of a Greek temple to Ares. Perhaps Apollonius got his details here from a Hellenistic travel writer.

The island is still a sacred site today. At the summer festival that takes place on 20 May each year, thousands of Muslims come to pray for a long life, health, potency and children. Boats arrive at the landing stage and then there's a scramble up through the woods to the middle of the island to reach the ruins of a small Byzantine monastery on the site of the ancient Greek temple. The early accounts say that the black stone where the Argonauts prayed was preserved inside the temple: if so, it is now buried in undergrowth. Today, there is an alternative black stone for Muslim pilgrims down on the shore, a huge circular boulder, lapped by the waves, its crevices packed with folded prayers and wish cloths at festival time. As we pushed on, the birds rose again in clouds, screeching eerily.

TO THE BORDER

Two days later we crossed over to Georgia, at a border post tucked under a wooded, rain-soaked cliff. We then found ourselves travelling along the lovely subtropical coast of Georgia, past the great Byzantine fortifications of Gonieh, and soon arrived in Batumi, another early Greek colony. Batumi (whose name comes from the Greek meaning 'fine harbour') stands at the end of a wide and beautiful plain covered with trees and intersected by many streams. Behind us in the interior, terraced mountains backed the plain, with higher summits receding into the clouds.

Poor Georgia, a land rich in history and high civilization, has had a disastrous modern history. The Russian invasion of 1917 introduced Communist rule to the country, which has suffered further troubles since the collapse of the Soviet empire. Recently the war in Chechnya has spilled over the mountains, while her own separatist wars threaten to break Georgia up: Abkhazia and South Ossetia are now in open warfare.

But when did the Greeks first come here? Some of the Greek communities on this coast go back to the sixth century BC, and continued to exist right through Roman and Byzantine times when this was an important far-flung eastern outpost for both empires. In modern times many came from Turkey in the nineteenth century, and then again after the disaster of 1922. With *perestroika* and the collapse of Communist rule here in 1993, ten thousand Greeks were lifted out by the Greek government in Operation Golden Fleece. But a large number are still here, living

Opposite: The 'Island of Ares', near Giresun, today. Here, opposite the coast of Amazons, the Argonauts were attacked by arrow-shooting birds. The island is still a pilgrimage place today.

in scattered villages tucked away in lovely countryside. This is wonderfully green, with an abundance of fecund fruit orchards, lush vineyards and lemon, orange and mandarin groves. Above the coast we wound our way up a dirt track to Dagva. Twenty years ago there were 2500 Greeks here, mainly from Pontus; now there are only 120. They have a loyalty to Greek culture – but they can't go back. 'We have no country of our own. We are like a pile of leaves, blown by the wind,' said one old man. 'We are children of Greece, but our great civilization is a broken mirror and we are one of the pieces.'

The village hall is a monument to that story: a huge mock-Greek temple from the Stalinist era, decorated with Greek script. The nearby Orthodox church, restored after being bombed by the Bolsheviks, has Greek icons and prayers round the dome. Later, at a family home up a farm track in the hills above Dagva, we toasted each other in local brandy, looking at some old photographs. One was of a village festival in August 1937, and with its Pontic costumes and lyre player it could have been a scene from ancient Greece. I narrowed my eyes, and there in black-and-white one could almost imagine Jason and Medea themselves.

Opposite: Sharing memories with today's Greek community in Dagva, Georgia.
Above: The lush, subtropical hills above Batumi on the Black Sea coast of Georgia were first settled by Greeks in the sixth century BC.

INTO THE PHASIS

> Then at last they reached the broad estuary of the Phasis, where the
> Black Sea ends, and they lowered their sail, and stowed the mast and
> yards, and rowed into that mighty river …
> APOLLONIUS OF RHODES *The Voyage of Argo c.* 250 BC

To get to the place where Jason landed in the myth you have to travel along the sea road across the coastal plain, past Soviet-era hotels and beach villas to Georgia's main modern port, Poti. Here it is easy to get a boat up the coast for the last few kilometres to the mouth of the river Rhion, the ancient Phasis. Getting into the river is not easy today, however, as seagoing boats no longer use it and sandbanks block its three main mouths. We ran aground twice, and one of our crew had to plunge in with a plumbing rod and wade through the surf, trying to find a channel through the sandbars. Finally we arrived in a wide flat estuary and chugged sedately between riverbanks as the sun set. Bathed in a golden light we saw freshwater turtles in the river, wild boar snuffling in the thickets and, above us, a great skein of migrating geese. Then, just before sunset, a strange vision appeared as a herd of fleet-footed brown horses, and just one pure white one, rushed past towards the sun. I was reminded of the myth of Aietes and the horses pulling the Sun God's chariot.

Apollonius had pictured on the left hand the 'lofty mountains of the Caucasus', and on the right the plain of Ares and the garden of Hecate. This was poetic licence. From where we were the snow-covered peaks of the Caucasus were out of sight far to the north. But southwards we could make out the mountains of Anatolia, and in front the wide green fertile plain where Greek mythographers imagined the city of Aia and the sacred grove with the tree and the Golden Fleece, guarded by the unsleeping dragon.

> So Jason poured a libation from a golden cup to the Earth, and to the
> gods of the land and its heroes, asking them to give him friendly help
> and happy anchorage. Then they rowed into the depth of the reedy
> marshes, moored the ship, cast the anchor stones, and passed the night
> in anxious expectation of the dawn.
> APOLLONIUS OF RHODES *The Voyage of Argo c.* 250 BC

Dawn over Lake Paliostomi: a vast wetland, with fishermen casting their nets, a network of waterways behind the coastal strip opening into wide lakes, a strange semiaquatic world over which the sun rises. It is a place to lose orientation. Here by the river, the story goes, the Argonauts hold their council of war. They have achieved their first goal, the epic journey. But what will they do now? After the council they decide to walk upriver from the *Argo* towards the city of Aia. On the way they encounter the first strange intimations of the topsy-turvy world of the land of Colchis in the form of dead bodies wrapped in hides and hung in trees. The strange fact is that this really did happen in ancient Colchis. Travellers to Georgia in the seventeenth century recount something similar: men killed by lightning were indeed hung in skins in trees, not committed to the earth. Evidence from the early Iron Age has suggested to Georgian archaeologists that it was the custom then for corpses to be exposed and picked clean by birds. So this weird detail in the myth seems to be a genuine piece of Colchian folklore, which Apollonius may have got from an older account. Maybe much older?

VANI: CITY OF GOLD

But where was Aietes' town? It was described by Apollonius in Homeric terms, with broad gates and lines of pillars along its walls, and a central great door of shining metal. The lanes that approached it were surrounded by canopies of vines (as the plain of Georgia is today). Did it really exist? And, if so, when? Later Greeks knew of a 'great barbarian city' a few kilometres from the sea but modern archaeologists have yet to find it. In the marshy tracery of the tributaries of the river Rhion more than twenty ancient sites have been located, up to 30 kilometres inland in a fertile landscape rich in timber and cattle and famous for the medicinal herbs that figure so prominently in the myth. But we shouldn't take Greek accounts of the city too literally. Aia, as we have it, is a fantasy world created by the classical Greeks with touches of Homer, touches of travellers' tales. As for a real Colchian city, we have no means of knowing whether the Greeks knew anything about the culture here much before 600 to 550 BC, when the first Greek colony was founded on the banks of the Phasis. That the myth might bear any relation whatsoever to late Bronze Age culture in the fourteenth and thirteenth centuries BC seems virtually impossible. It is more likely to describe the historical Iron Age kingdom of Colchis, some of whose towns the Greeks might actually have seen. And the most important of these is Vani.

Overleaf: The plains of Georgia behind the coastal waterlands of Lake Paliostomi. The Iron Age city of Vani, set back in these hills, is perhaps where the classical Greeks imagined the city of the Golden Fleece.

In 1876 local Georgian newspapers reported treasures washed from a mysterious wooded hill in the foothills above the river Rhion, 30 kilometres in from the sea. Golden necklaces, armlets and earrings found their way into the hands of collectors. The hill of gold commanded a fine view over the river and the plain, and traces of ancient buildings lay near the summit below a ruined medieval church. Some antiquarians suggested that this might be the site of the Argonaut legend. Even the great Heinrich Schliemann, the excavator of Troy and Mycenae, with his unerring touch for sifting out the truth behind myths, hoped to find the city of the Golden Fleece and proposed to dig there. After the Jewels of Helen and the Mask of Agamemnon, did he maybe think he might even turn up the Fleece itself?! However, perhaps aware of Schliemann's reputation as a con man, charlatan and smuggler of antiquities, the tsar's government refused him permission.

As it turned out Schliemann's instinct, as always, was right. Excavations since 1947 have shown that, between 600 and 400 BC, as the legend took final shape, Vani must have been the city the early Greeks knew when they first established their trading colony on the coast. Though not occupied in the Heroic Age in which the myth is set, it was the native Colchian capital at the time when the Greek poets located the myth by the river Phasis. On the hill there are stone defences, shrines and open-air altars. There is also a statue of the 'goddess at the gate' – interestingly echoed in a late version of the myth which describes Artemis as the 'guardian of gates' – standing beside the entrance to the city of Aia. And there is also gold, lots of it. Remarkable finds include gold ornaments decorated with motifs reaching deep into the past of Colchis, such as the turtles of Lake Paliostomi, birds and golden rams. These recur on necklaces, earrings and plaques – sunbursts and golden rams in the land of the sun. If its barbaric splendour sparks our imagination, it certainly did that of the ancient Greeks.

ENTER MEDEA

In Vani, then, perhaps the classical Greeks imagined the royal hall at Aia. In the story, Jason asks Aietes outright for the return of the Fleece, which had once belonged to Jason's ancestors, a gift from Zeus. Aietes says that to get it Jason must perform a series of superhuman tasks. He must yoke fire-breathing bulls, plough and sow a field with dragons' teeth, and then overcome the phantom warriors who will arise from the furrows – impossible tasks. But the king's daughter, Medea, has fallen in love with Jason (as women do), and she is a priestess, a spell worker, and

the granddaughter of Helios, the Sun God. She can help him achieve the tasks – but only if he will take her as his wife. Jason agrees immediately. His line of fate is beginning to appear.

Now we enter a deeper level of the legend both psychologically and in terms of the layers of the story. Jason has accomplished the heroic voyage to Colchis, and so far it has been a simple tale of the hero's quest. This fairy-tale now becomes much more complicated. Indeed, a whole new story emerges and a new pro-tagonist enters the tale who will become one of the foremost figures in Greek myth, and one of the most powerful female figures in all literature: the daughter of Aietes – Medea.

Jason only gets the Fleece with the help of Medea, who becomes his lover and wife but whom he then rejects, and who in the end will destroy him. The story takes different forms, and the role of Medea has been hotly argued. Is she a pure

Above: Current excavations at Vani. Georgian archaeologists have uncovered a rich fortified city from between 600 and 400 BC, which may be the one remembered by Greek tradition as the city of the Sun God.

Greek invention, or could she be a reflection, however distant, of early Colchian culture? Is she part of the original story or a later addition? Or is she even nothing to do with the original tale, but a character in Corinthian culture only later identified with the Colchian story by a Corinthian poet around 700 BC?

Medea's role is that of the divine female helper, who plays a part in so many myths down the ages. Fascinating new evidence suggests that Medea may belong to the deeper levels of the tale – conceivably even its Bronze Age core. The evidence takes us away from Georgia to a site that is 200 kilometres inland from the Black Sea coast of Turkey and one of the most important archaeological digs of the twentieth century.

THE HERO, THE GODDESS AND THE DRAGON

The excavations at Boghaz Köy in central Turkey in the 1920s and 1930s uncovered the remains of the lost civilization of the Hittite empire. At the time of the Heroic Age in Greece, the Hittites ruled from Syria to the Aegean, engaged in diplomacy with Egypt and Babylonia, and seem to have clashed with a Mycenaean Greek king in the region of Troy. Hoards of tablets were discovered, inscribed with the earliest specimens of an Indo-European language, earlier even than the first surviving specimens of Greek, Old Persian or Sanskrit. They contained treaties, letters, annals, ritual texts, myths and stories. When the first myths were translated, scholars were excited to see that some of these texts, dating from the fourteenth century BC and earlier, bore a striking resemblance to Greek myths recorded many centuries later. Recently it was noticed that one of these throws fascinating light on the Jason myth, and gives us unprecedented insight into the possible prehistory of the Greek myth in a completely unexpected analogy for the tale.

The story of the hero Hupasiyas, the dragon Illuyankas and the goddess Inaras survives in a text from around 1400 BC. It was performed in the New Year spring festival, in a fertility ritual similar not only to those of ancient Egypt and Babylon, but also to the fights with a dragon acted out in Europe on St George's Day right up to the twentieth century. There are two versions, both of which have a tragic and frightening dimension that crosses the boundary from ritual text into literature and myth, and both curiously resonate with themes in the Jason myth.

Opposite: *Medea* by Frederick Augustus Sandys. One of the great figures in Greek myth, it is unclear whether she was part of the original (late Bronze Age?) story.

In the first version, already old in 1400 BC and 'the one they no longer tell', the storm god chooses a mortal hero to fight a seemingly invincible dragon, which even the gods cannot overthrow. The hero agrees to this but on condition that the goddess will become his lover. The goddess becomes the hero's lover but demands that in return he never look again at his wife and children. With the help of the goddess, the mortal then overcomes the dragon and goes to live with her. But he breaks his bond when he looks again on his wife and children from the window of the goddess's secret chamber; in her jealousy she destroys him.

The second version gives an even more intriguing slant on the story. This is the version 'they told later', the one enacted or retold in the spring festivals around 1400 BC. Here the hero is half mortal, half divine, having been born of a mortal mother. On his quest he goes to the dragon's lair and takes the daughter of the dragon as his wife. He then betrays the hospitality of his father-in-law by enabling the gods to kill the dragon. In an almost tragic paradox he himself is killed because he broke the law of the guest. 'Kill me too!' he shouts at the end. 'Show no compassion for me!' The gods therefore punish and kill him too, even though he has a divine father.

The essential triangle in this story has existed from the very beginnings of myth. The theme of a hero, a dark power and a beautiful female helper, who is often the daughter or lover of the hero's enemy, forms the pattern in stories all the way down to the James Bond films. This might suggest that the hero and his divine lover, the dragon and the wicked father or host, are not late additions to the story. It is not known how or when such myths were borrowed by the Greeks, but that there was a transmission seems clear. This idea fits very well with exciting recent discoveries showing affinities between Near Eastern poetry and the Homeric poems – some of the most obvious being in the role of gods and goddesses. In this light it is worth remembering that Aia, the land of the Sun God in Greek myth, is the name of the Sun God's wife in Hittite and earlier Near Eastern and Mesopotamian myths.

Two alternative explanations may be suggested for when the tale was borrowed into the Greek bardic tradition. First, it could have been in the late Mycenaean Age itself – the Heroic Age, the time in which tradition places the tales of Jason and Troy. Alternatively it may have been borrowed in the ninth or eighth centuries BC, during what has become known as the 'orientalizing revolution', when many themes seem to have come into Greek poetry from the east, via Syria, Cilicia, Anatolia, Cyprus and Rhodes. The second theory is much more likely, if similar borrowings in Homer are anything to go by. If this is the case, it might be that the theme of the mortal who rejects his superior wife in favour of a goddess who helps him kill a dragon is the part of the myth that, in the century or two before Homer, was added to the original late Bronze Age adventure of the Prince of Iolkos.

The long-lost prehistory of the myth is beginning to resurface. So what then of the Golden Fleece itself? As we have seen, Hittite texts show that in their New Year festival sacred fleeces – 'fleeces of the sun' – were hung on tree totems in the temple. Could the Fleece too be a memory of a real cult practice from the Bronze Age? On my journey it was time to pursue the Fleece itself.

SVANETI: THE SEARCH FOR THE FLEECE

His body protected by a magic ointment given to him by Medea, Jason braves the fire-breathing bulls, sows the dragons' teeth and overcomes the phantom warriors by throwing a stone in their midst, over which they fight and kill each other. The tasks fulfilled, he claims the Fleece. Aietes pretends to agree, and throws a great banquet, but secretly he intends to burn the *Argo* and kill the Argonauts. Medea, however, reveals her father's plans to Jason, and they immediately go to the sacred grove together to confront the dragon which guards the Fleece.

To pursue the story of the Fleece – and more particularly the meaning of the Fleece – we left the Black Sea coast of Georgia and set off into the wild gorges of Svaneti in the Caucasus mountains. My hope was to test an ancient tale that has become a modern legend. The story appears to begin with Strabo, the first-century geographer, who attempted to explain the Golden Fleece by pure rational anthropology:

> It is said that in the country of Colchis, gold is carried down by the mountain torrents, and that the barbarians obtain it by means of perforated troughs and fleecy skins, and that this is the origin of the myth of the Golden Fleece.

Ever since, Strabo's theory has stuck and Georgians insist that the Fleece story came from the gold-bearing rivers of Svaneti. Travel writers, journalists and film-makers alike have willed it to be true, and mounted convincing scenes of panning for gold with fleeces. Though sceptical myself, I felt I had to check it out.

We drove for several hours up the Svaneti valley, and were soon surrounded by the snowy peaks of the Caucasus mountains which run along the border with Ossetia and Chechnya. Each village we passed through welcomed us, offering up

toasts with rocket-fuel vodka, for this is a drinking culture. Drinking here is an essential ritual of friendship: 'Tonight we must drink as men,' they say, and there are touching, affectionate toasts from the old to the young: 'May you replace me.' I was reminded of a strange passage in Herodotus about a Scythian tribe who were convinced that 'drinking companions and their descendants would not die'. Membership of the clan and participation in festive eating and drinking would guarantee your hopes for the next world. The same, of course, was true in Greek culture. Witness the staggering array of drinking utensils in the Macedonian royal tombs and the role of drink in Alexander's court. Drinking was a kind of initiation, and through drinking the guest outsider was temporarily co-opted into the group. Drinking determined your status in the here and now and, in archaic belief, helped your status after death too. It is easy to understand how in a society on the edge of violence, surrounded by inscrutable forces, festive drinking took on a vital role.

Night had fallen by the time we reached Mestia, an extraordinary cluster of medieval towers, some going back to the seventh century. Buildings such as these began to be constructed in the last centuries BC, when culture developed in this area, and a trade route opened up into the Caucasus. Greek coins have turned up here bearing the images of Philip and Alexander and their successors, thus dating from the time when the tale of the Fleece was being told in faraway Alexandria. Svaneti has deep connections with the pagan world of pre-Christian Georgia. Near Mestia, the Georgian version of the myth of Prometheus appears on a church wall, accompanied by the image of the hero and the dragon. On the church walls, there were stone rams' heads, on the altars horns of consecration from sacrificed rams and bulls. Outside clouds scudded over the snowy peaks of the Caucasus.

The next day we went up to find the gold panners. In a village above Mestia we found a prospector who showed us tiny gold nuggets made from the grains he had panned. On the river he demonstrated the old method of panning. Calf, goat or sheep fleeces were used, he explained, which caught the fine gold-bearing silt in their hair. Strabo's story, then, seems to have some truth in it after all; but as an explanation of the myth it is, to my mind, still implausible. As we shall see, the legend of the Fleece has far deeper, older – and stranger – roots.

Opposite: The Svaneti valley running up to the Caucasus mountains on the border with Ossetia.
Overleaf: The Caucasus mountains. To the classical Greeks this was the edge of the known world, where the Titan Prometheus was crucified by Zeus for giving fire to humankind – a myth that has survived in Georgia until today.

IN THE SACRED GROVE

That night we returned to Mestia where we heard spine-tingling polyphonic singing: not a Christian hymn but one addressed to the sun, for, as one of the singers said, 'The sun is a god.' More echoes of the ancient world.

So we come to the climax of Jason's quest for the Fleece. Medea leads him into the sacred grove. Coiled round the tree is a terrifying serpent, 'thicker and longer than a ship with fifty oars ... with glaring eyes and bright scales'. The various surviving representations of the tale in poetry and art suggest that other versions once existed. One extraordinary vase painting even shows Jason being regurgitated by the dragon, having been swallowed, like Jonah was by the whale. In one version, Jason kills the monster; in Apollonius, Medea drugs the dragon

Above and opposite: A fortified village near Mestia, the chief town in the Svaneti valley. These medieval tower houses were built by local clans for defence in a culture riven by blood feud and revenge killing.

with another of her potions, Jason climbs the tree and finally takes the Fleece into his hands.

So what is the meaning of the Golden Fleece, hanging in its sacred grove? That question takes us on one last journey. We are on the Georgian military highway heading up towards the Caucasus mountains bordering Chechnya. This is a land of ancient gods. Here isolated tribes still worship pagan deities and even Christians inhabit a world soaked in pagan custom. In the village of the gold panners the women had told us tales of Medea: how the Greeks took her by force, and how here in Georgia there are still women like her, 'oracle women', who have always existed in Georgian society. We are hoping now to find the women oracles

Above: Traditional Georgian singers at a supra, or toasting feast, in Mestia. They specialize in the polyphonic singing of ancient songs, some of which hark back to a pagan past.

and their strange pagan world of the Caucasus which coexists alongside the war-torn reality of the twenty-first century.

In the last part of my search I also hoped to find living traces of the Fleece cult itself. My notebook by now was filled with a weird series of stories, from modern Greek folk belief and Roman oracles to ancient Hittite rituals in which fleeces were hung on trees in temples to greet the spring. Apollonius's description of the Fleece conveys its magical aura: 'thick piled, glowing with matted skeins of gold.' Up here, I was told, I might see something of what this really meant.

We arrived at night after a long journey, and on the road after sunset we had to ask the way many times. As we entered a long valley in growing darkness, the mountains closed in all around us; we forded two swollen rivers and then headed up a grassy hillside through copses of trees. At last we saw campfires and pitched our tents. The next morning it was damp when we awoke after a night of dancing and music round the fires. At seven o'clock flagons of vodka were brought over for more festive drinking: to the gods, friendship and long life.

Below us lay a flat plateau above a wooded river valley full of summer flowers. Some distance down the slope, where the plateau falls away into the valley, are the shrines. We approach the sacred grove where a circular wall encloses several tall old trees. The main shrine is to St George, but there are others – all dripping with burning candles and tapers. On the branches of the trees are hung knotted prayer cloths. Rams and sheep are sacrificed on the grass outside the enclosure wall. The priest blesses them, touching each animal almost tenderly, then its head is hacked off with a Georgian sword. The grass is soaked in blood; heads are scattered among the trees; there are horns and fleeces on the wall of the shrine. People circle anti-clockwise offering prayers, while all through the day rams are brought to be blessed and killed.

Later that day the women oracles finally arrived. There were fifteen or twenty of them, accompanied by a few of their menfolk and some children. They camped under the trees with their cooking pots and threw up a big communal tent, open on one side. By now the sun was hot. The women tell the future, cure people with herbs (but not if you have already been touched by a Western doctor) and perform incantation magic – sometimes entering trances so strenuous that they make themselves ill. In the old days – even during Communist times according to an early anthropologist's account – their rituals were strongly pagan. Now they have been co-opted into the Christian world. The leader raises her arms and prayers are said to St George, Mary Magdalene and the angels, Lashari and Queen Tamar. A drone rises up: 'Bring us peace, free us from violence, release us from troubles.'

As I watched rams being led to be sacrificed, and saw their heads and shorn fleeces displayed on the wall of the shrine, my mind went back to the grove of Ares and the Queen of the Night, Hecate, in the myth of the *Argo*. The rituals of all the early religions were essentially the same: there is a remarkable similarity, for example, between animal sacrifices in ancient Babylonia and Greece. Even today Muslims still perform animal sacrifices at Mecca itself. Killing and sacredness have gone hand in hand throughout history. Homo Ludens (the player) is also Homo Necans (the killer). Perhaps the Fleece was part of the original story too?

After the killing was over we put the camera away and sat down with the oracle women to enjoy their Sunday feast under the trees, bathed in warm sunshine. We sat on logs making our inevitable toasts – to the women this time, for this was the women's world. And I felt I was touching on the last remnant of the deep culture that had been shared by the people of the Bronze Age Aegean and the mountain people of prehistoric Anatolia and the Caucasus: the world in which the myth had grown.

THE RETURN TO GREECE

So Jason takes the Fleece; he and Medea make love by the banks of the Phasis and he swears by the almighty gods that he will be faithful to her for ever. Then they rush to the *Argo*, which is ready to sail. The expedition to Colchis is almost over.

As for our journey, we returned to the coast near Poti on a wonderful midsummer's night. On a long rolling shore, an immense beach of black sand, lay a tide of flotsam washed down by the currents of the rivers of Russia. In the last golden light, kids played in the blackened skeleton of a Soviet-era hotel. Somewhere near here the myth sets the Argonauts' departure, and Medea's dismembering of her own younger brother to delay the pursuers – a chilling foretaste of things to come.

There are several different versions of the return of the *Argo*, which reflect different stages of Greek geographical knowledge. In one of the earliest, Pindar hints that the Argonauts sailed *up* the Phasis, which was seen as a kind of canal to the Great Ocean, and then circled the world southwards. 'They came to the depths of Ocean, to the Red Sea,' he says, and then carried the *Argo* overland across Libya – as one commentator put it, 'to our sea'. In another version the Greeks sail from the Phasis, into the Don (Tanais) and this time sail north to the Ocean, then sail through 'The Frozen Sea', past the British Isles (Ierne) and enter the Mediterranean through the Strait of Gibraltar. Apollonius, on the other hand, takes them on a fantasy voyage up the Danube, and overland into the Adriatic.

These versions cannot be reconciled, nor do the ancient authorities attempt to do so. We are left with the *Argo*'s track, a distant sail, and faint sea marks against a molten sunset. They sail home with the Fleece.

And there you might have thought the story ended – they go back, have lots of children and live happily ever after? But, of course, Greek myths are not like that. Or at least not the Greek myths as they are told by the great tragedians and poets. Mortals don't live happily ever after, only gods do that. You can be a darling of the goddess, you can fulfil the oracles, kill dragons, lead a charmed life, but if you fail to show due respect to the gods and humans, and if you break your solemn vows – then your true destiny will be revealed.

JASON'S DESTINY

Back in Iolkos, Jason presents Pelias with the Fleece and claims the kingdom, but then dark forces seem to crowd in. Medea tells the daughters of King Pelias that with her magic powers she can rejuvenate him, and she convinces them to dismember their father like a ram at sacrifice. Medea and Jason and their young children are driven out of Iolkos and go into exile in Corinth. There the king offers Jason his daughter, and, disastrously, Jason agrees to marry her. As Medea is no ordinary human woman, so her passions are correspondingly great. In revenge she puts a magic cloak on the bride which cannot be taken off, and burns her to death. Then, in the ultimate horror, she kills her and Jason's children. The Roman playwright Seneca's version of the tale ends with the tremendous, hopeless cry of her broken husband: 'Go where you will across the high spaces of heaven. But bear witness that, wherever you are, there are no gods.'

THE HORROR

From the Corinth road you walk on a narrow dirt track through an olive grove down the promontory towards the lighthouse, a heavenly spot overlooking the Gulf of Corinth and with a majestic view towards Delphi and Parnassos. In his first-century guidebook to Greece, the Greek writer Pausanias describes a mysterious shrine to the murdered children of Jason and Medea at Corinth. It lay in the vicinity of a temple to Hera Akraia ('Hera of the heights'), the protectress of Jason. Close by was a 'most frightful statue of a woman' whom he does not name but calls simply 'the horror'. Other ancient sources say that Medea herself was the founder of the Hera cult here, in memory of her children.

Until the early 1930s it was thought that these enigmatic monuments stood inside the city of Corinth itself. Then a British excavation at Perachora, across the bay from the city, put a different perspective on the story. Right under a little rural chapel an archaic temple to Hera Akraia was discovered, going back at least as far as the eighth century BC. Close by was a sacred pool and an oracle site, with huge numbers of pilgrims' offerings (especially it would seem from women), running right through to Roman times.

So had the shrine to Medea's dead children actually been here, outside the city where legend says the murder took place? And was it part of the Corinthian cult of Hera Akraia, which is specifically connected with the Medea myth by Euripides and other fifth-century BC tragedians?

At the end, then, there is a grim irony. Medea becomes a female demon, the kind that we find in folk tales across the Mediterranean and beyond – like La Lorona, the 'Weeping Woman', in Mexican belief. She is the spirit of a mother, who, having murdered her own children, spends eternity wandering the earth looking for others to kill. She is the 'terror', the female transgressor, the irrational or inexplicable child killer, confined here in her place so she that she may be propitiated by all who see in her their own secret fears.

As for Jason, he ends up becoming what he was at the start: a man alone in the world, a wanderer with one shoe. Finally he goes back to the thing that gave him his fame – the *Argo* itself. The decaying wreck of his old boat was now on display in Iolkos. There, Jason meets his death when the speaking beam from the magic oak of Dodona falls on him as he sits weeping in its shadow. The story has come full circle: made by the gods, destroyed by the gods, Jason's destiny has been revealed.

EPILOGUE: THE HERO'S QUEST

> Glory! Your fire warms men's souls as it quickens their hearts and minds. He can see your ghostly figure beckoning there in the distant mists of the Phasis valley; he can hear that siren's song that inspires men to risk their all. Are they heroes? Or mere dreamers?
> VALERIUS FLACCUS *The Voyage of the Argo* c. AD 90.

Previous pages: Perachora, across the gulf from Corinth, with the temple of Hera, dating from before 800 BC, by the shore. Tradition said it was founded by Medea in the place where her murdered children were commemorated.

Where the story of Jason was first told we will never know. Perhaps the point about myths is that they are tales that are never told for the first time? But the legend of the voyage of a prince of Iolkos to a magic land was perhaps already being recited in Thessaly at the end of the Bronze Age, maybe even around the great hearth in the royal hall so recently found at Dimini. The account of the voyage of the *Argo*, and the adventures of its crew of heroes, would have been part of a cycle of poems sung by the bards, along with tales of other kings, such as Pelias, and perhaps even the feats of that other Thessalian hero Achilles. These were fitting stories to be sung to the lyre around the fire after the feasting, tales of the greatest heroes and the most thrilling deeds. Whether there ever was a real voyage will remain a mystery, though, as we have seen, it is not impossible that Bronze Age or early Iron Age Greek sailors entered the Black Sea and played their part in the shaping of the myth. But the enduring appeal of the tale over three thousand years does not come from any possible historical core, but from its enduring power as a myth of the hero's quest, its pessimistic view of human destiny and its insistence on the undying fame that the hero wins through his glorious deeds.

THE QUEEN
OF SHEBA

Wisdom is my daughter, for whose sake the Queen of the South
came out of the East like the rising dawn, in order to hear, understand
and behold the wisdom of Solomon. Power, honour, strength and
dominion are given into her hands; she wears the royal cloak of seven
glittering stars, like a bride adorned for her husband, and on her
robe is written in golden lettering, in Greek, Arabic and Latin:
'I am the only daughter of the wise; utterly unknown to the foolish.'

From an early fourteenth-century text attributed to ST THOMAS AQUINAS

EASTER NIGHT IN JERUSALEM. A pale half moon silvers the clouds above
Gethsemane. Over the city the golden dome floats like an ethereal vision in the
blue twilight. City of legend and city of dreams, for which people have lived and
died for thousands of years: Jews, Christians and Muslims; Greeks, Romans
and Saracens; Alexander, Saladin, Tamburlaine. There are few places on earth
as soaked in history, and in myth. There's Adam's grave on Golgotha; the temple

Previous pages: The landscape near Yeha in Ethiopia – the heartland of humanity.
Opposite: The visit of the Queen of Sheba to Solomon depicted in a thirteenth-century French manuscript. Her story became very popular in Europe after the crusades as a parable of the pagan world accepting the Scriptures.
Above: Easter night in Jerusalem. Ethiopian pilgrims on their way to the Church of the Holy Sepulchre.

of Solomon; Christ's Calvary; and the site of the Prophet Muhammad's ascent to heaven; the tour guides can even point the modern-day pilgrim to the omphalos itself – the navel of the earth. Tonight crowds jam the narrow streets in the Coptic quarter, shuffling past the souvenir shops and the kebab stalls, pushing into the little lane that leads to the courtyard of the Holy Sepulchre. Inside the church, which is heavy with the scent of incense, women wring their perfumed cloths over the glistening marble slab where legend says the body of Jesus was laid. Under the great rotunda queues wait to enter the tiny marble chamber where he was buried; and behind us mysterious corridors echo with the vast susurration of the pilgrims. Shadowy stairways plunge into a darkness pierced only by pinpricks of lamplight, a cavernous underworld where candles flicker in front of blackened icons, and ancient flagstones receive the tears of the faithful.

Tucked away by the Calvary steps, a narrow passageway leads along the side of the Holy Sepulchre into a little church where hundreds of African pilgrims listen to prayers in their own language, Geez. They are Ethiopians – here, as always, even though theirs is one of the poorest countries on earth. Most of them are women, wearing long white cotton dresses and cloaks, and white turbans. They all carry burning tapers, which light up their eyes and their ebony faces. The beauty of it all takes the breath away. Above their heads in the nave is a huge painting, not of Christ, but of the Queen of Sheba standing before Solomon with bales of incense, elephant tusks and other treasures of Africa.

Next to me, a woman from Addis Ababa explains that their link with the Holy Land goes back far beyond the days when Ethiopia became a Christian state in the time of the late Roman empire. The first contact was made all of three thousand years ago: 'There are many stories about her, but we believe, and we know, that the queen came from Ethiopia. She came searching for wisdom: she was a seeker after truth. She was a powerful woman, beautiful and strong and wise. And she tested Solomon with hard questions. And they fell in love. She had a son by him called Menelik, who was the first of the line of kings of Ethiopia right down to Ras Tafari, Haile Selassie himself. And Solomon showed Sheba his temple and taught her about his religion, and she followed him in worshipping the true God, which the Ethiopians have done ever since. The tale is about religion. But it is also about love.'

She smiles, her eyes flashing in the candlelight. 'Not all things happen in history because of war, violence and conquest, you know.'

MYTHS AND LEGENDS IN THE BIBLE

> The Queen of Sheba heard of the fame of King Solomon and wished
> to test him with riddles. She arrived in Jerusalem with a very large
> retinue and with camels bearing incense, a great quantity of gold and
> precious stones ... and there never came such abundance of spices as
> those which the Queen of Sheba gave to King Solomon.
>
> 1 Kings 10:1–2, 10

Among all the famous story-tellers in the world, along with the Celts, the Greeks and the Indians, the Jews have left one of the greatest legacies. The Bible tales were written down in the late Iron Age and into the period of Persian and Greek rule in the Near East (600–200 BC). They have proved amazingly tenacious and enduring, and have had an extraordinary impact on the history of civilization because of their importance to the three monotheistic religions. The tales of Solomon and the Queen of Sheba, after all, even provide the founding myths for two modern states: Israel and Ethiopia.

The first appearance of the tale of the Queen of Sheba's visit to King Solomon in Jerusalem is a short narrative in the Old Testament, which has so far proved impossible to verify as history. However, the tale is elaborated in sometimes fantastic detail in a vast body of later literature. It is found in Jewish, Muslim and Christian stories, in Turkish and Persian painting, in Kabbalistic treatises and in medieval Christian alchemical and mystical works, where the queen is viewed as the embodiment of Divine Wisdom, a prophet of Christ and a foreteller of the cult of the Holy Cross. In modern novels and movies she has enjoyed a curious and varied afterlife as a cultural icon, Rastafarian saint and orientalist fantasy. Today, her statue still stands next to that of Solomon on the front of the great cathedral at Chartres in France, while in the sacred books of the Ethiopian Orthodox Church the queen is viewed literally as the mother of the nation, whose son brought the Lost Ark of the Covenant back to Axum – where it still resides today!

The Queen of Sheba is a fascinating case of a famous myth whose hero is a woman. The story of her various reinventions over the centuries is a tale in itself, but what is also intriguing about her is the history that the Bible story seems to imply – the existence of far-flung trade routes between the Holy Land, the Incense Coast and the Horn of Africa. The luxuries that the queen brought to Solomon, such as the finest incense, are hints that place the story in the great opening

up of the world to long-distance commerce in the first millennium BC. This was a time that has left us some of the most fascinating historical documents from the ancient world.

On one level, therefore, this journey in search of the Queen of Sheba is an exploration of a myth, but on another it is an investigation of the real historical links that connected early Arabia with the Near East and Africa. It takes us to two spectacular ancient civilizations, which are still barely known to the outside world: the lost Ethiopian empire of Axum (the first civilization of sub-Saharan Africa) and the kingdom of Saba in Yemen (the first civilization of early Arabia). But it is also a quest for a phantom, a woman with no name, and yet with many names: Makeda and Azeb, Bilkis and Balmaka, Nikaulis, Kandake, Sibilla – all of these are the Queen of Sheba.

Above: A detail from Tomasso's *Triumphal Procession of the Queen of Sheba*, fifteenth century.
Opposite: An Ethiopian miniature depicting Solomon and Sheba – the kind of popular art sold as a pilgrim's souvenir on paintings, scarves and vellum.

THE BIBLE STORY

'I'd be very careful about historical kernels if I were you,' said Yair Zakovitch with a twinkle in his eye. 'The whole story sounds very much like a fairy-tale to me.'

We were in the conservation lab of the National Library in Jerusalem; in our hands was the most ancient and precious Bible manuscript in existence. The Aleppo codex was saved from the destruction of the old synagogue in Aleppo in Syria in 1948 during the violence that flamed across the Arab world at the time of the founding of Israel. This is the oldest surviving Hebrew text of the Bible, written in the tenth century AD, though there are earlier manuscripts of the Greek translation.

Yair turned to the account in 1 Kings and began to read softly: 'This is Hebrew any Jewish child could understand today,' he remarked. 'When she came to Solomon she asked him all that was on her mind, and he satisfied all her desires.' I can't take my eyes off the manuscript. The first impression? Crisp, creamy parchment and faded brown ink carefully annotated with accent and breathing marks: a real text by a real writer whose name appears in a colophon. No text in human history has had to bear more weight; wars have been fought over it, and civilizations ravaged in crusades old and new.

It didn't come down from the sky, however. Its various parts were first composed and recorded at different times in the centuries before Christ. So when was the account of King Solomon written? The question raises the problem faced by anyone using the early parts of the Bible to retrieve historical facts. They were written down, most scholars agree, centuries after the purported events they describe, probably starting in the sixth century BC before the Jewish exile in Babylonia. But the texts we have today are the end products of a standardizing by rabbinical editors, which occurred between the sixth and ninth centuries AD. Solomon is traditionally dated back to the tenth century BC. It is not surprising that with such a gap in time, fierce controversy has arisen between those who think the material they contain is basically historical, those who view it as largely mythic and those who look for kernels – historical or otherwise.

Yair was warming to his theme: 'Look, Solomon in the Bible is presented as a kind of wunderkind, and the material is put into Kings to glorify him. All the kings of the world come to admire him and the wealth of the world is brought to his court. The Queen of Sheba story is one of those where there are clearly already mythic elements which may go back to earlier stories. Take the riddles, for example: she asks him hard questions. Well, this kind of riddle contest appears in folk tales in many cultures as a kind of battle of the sexes, often as part of a marriage negotiation. There was probably much more that the rabbis left out. He satisfied all her desires in addition to what he gave her in his official capacity as king. Well, Solomon had many wives, and is criticized in Jewish sources for being too addicted to women. But she was not a wife, and perhaps for that reason the implied sexual liaison is not mentioned.'

It is hard not to agree with Yair about the fairy-tale elements. In the Bible, Sheba represents the far south more as a mental construct than as a real place. It is a land of luxury and sensual pleasures, and the queen herself embodies a submissive and voluptuous orient; a territory of the imagination, which later classical and Islamic sources elaborate into an exotic land of wonders. It is a land of otherness too, not least of blackness. And so it has been constructed right down to Hollywood and in popular literature till today. When the Queen of Sheba appears in Solomon's court in the Bible, she brings not only an abundance of rare incense and gold, but also helps inaugurate a myth of the Orient which in our own time has been so sharply dissected by, among others, the late Edward Said.

That said, and allowing for all the mythic elements, does a historical event lie behind the tale? If not, why should a queen of Sheba be mentioned at all? What we read as Sheba in the Bible (Hebrew *Shbwa*), though exotic and wondrous, clearly is a real place. There are many references in the Old Testament to the land and its people, in Genesis, Psalms, Isaiah, Jeremiah and Ezekiel. In the New Testament, Jesus invokes her as one of the just who will rise up to condemn unbelievers, identifying himself with Solomon, and 'the Queen of the South' with the Church, his divine spouse.

The geographical position of Sheba, however, has always been contentious. From the Bible references most scholars believe the name means Saba, which was the important Iron Age kingdom of South Arabia. On the other hand the Bible also knows a Seba in Africa, which was identified with Cush, or Ethiopia; and the Roman Jewish scholar Josephus says that in his day the queen was believed to be African, a queen of the Ethiopians, and this line is followed today by the Ethiopian Church.

Yair's advice about historical kernels is therefore very much to the point, as with all the stories in this book. But is there a real historical context to the tale? And why has the story had such an extraordinary afterlife? To find that out, first we need to answer the important question: when did Solomon reign?

Overleaf: The Dome of the Rock in Jerusalem with the modern city in the background. Few places in the world are more soaked in religion and myth – or have been more fought over.

THE BIBLE AND HISTORY

'Well, to answer that question you need good primary evidence from texts, inscriptions and archaeology,' said Israel Finkelstein.

'So is there any?' I asked.

He laughed. 'No.'

We were walking on the beach below Jaffa, the old Mediterranean port for Jerusalem. Affable and formidably in command of the material evidence, Finkelstein is an eminent archaeologist who has his own solution to the thorny field of biblical archaeology, and in particular the story in the Book of Kings that Solomon, son of David, ruled from the Euphrates to the frontier of Egypt.

Finkelstein continued: 'The problem is that as an archaeologist I can find no evidence for the great kingdom of Solomon that the Bible describes. What I see in the ground in the tenth century BC is a small chiefdom in the hills of Judaea. The kingdom of Solomon probably existed, but the kingdom described in the Bible looks to me like an exaggerated reflection of the situation in the eighth and seventh centuries BC. Especially all the detail about relations with other rulers in the Near East and further afield. In the early Iron Age the world was opening up, the empire of the Assyrians conquered the Near East, and with them you have a host of accurately dated texts which for the first time tell us about diplomatic relations between the Near East and Arabia. If I were going to look for the Queen of Sheba, I'd look in the eighth century, the Assyrian century, the first age of globalization.'

FROM PUNT TO SABA: THE INCENSE TRADE IN HISTORY

If the first clue is her name, the second is the incense: 'There never came such abundance of spices as those which the Queen of Sheba gave to King Solomon.' The Hebrew text uses the word for incense, one of the most precious substances in the ancient world, which was burned on the altars of the gods across the Near East and the Mediterranean. The name and the exotic gifts are inextricably bound up together in every version of the tale. The queen's gifts were frankincense and myrrh, the produce of Sheba, and there were – and are – only two places where incense bushes were cultivated for their precious aromatic sap: South Arabia, and the Ethiopian borderland with the Horn of Africa. These two regions, which have been closely connected for much of their history, are separated by less than 25 kilometres of water, and as it happens they are also the two places most strongly connected with the queen in the legend.

Stripped of its mythic overlays, then, the tale looks like a memory of an embassy by an Iron Age potentate bearing the produce of the Incense Coast to the Near Eastern world. And for that scenario we can immediately find a real context. Strange as it may sound in our materialist age, in the theocratic societies of the Bronze and Iron Age Levant, rulers and their élites were prepared to go to huge effort and expense to get hold of the rarest incense to burn before their gods, and it became a commodity almost as precious as gold. Astonishingly, records of the trade between the Horn of Africa and the Mediterranean go as far back as the mid-third millennium BC. These sources begin with references to journeys by the ancient Egyptians down the Red Sea to a mysterious land of incense called Punt. The trade with Punt was perhaps the first international long-distance commerce. In wall paintings from the fifteenth century BC in the temple of Hatshepsut near Luxor, large ocean-going vessels with thirty oars make the journey, sailing down the Red Sea to a place that is clearly identified by its flora and fauna (including giraffes

Above: Hatshepsut's mortuary temple on the West Bank near Luxor in Egypt. How extraordinary that one of the chief painted cycles on the temple's walls should be devoted to an account of a journey to the land of incense.

and baboons) as an East African habitat. Great heaps of incense taller than a man are shown, and incense trees are even dug up and carried to the ships in baskets, to be taken back to Egypt and planted in front of the temples there. In return, the Egyptians trade tools, weapons, clothes and textiles, preserved food, beer and wine. At the end of the voyage the Egyptian ruler Queen Hatshepsut – another woman of power – is seen offering incense to the Egyptian gods.

Now Egypt, of course, was the great culture of its day – the first great civilizing power in the world. But what is really fascinating is that the trade went the other way too: the Egyptians describe the rulers of Punt leading expeditions to Egypt on large, raft-like boats with lateen sails made of black material. So where precisely was Punt? In some cases it seems clear that in Egyptian eyes Punt meant what we call the coast of Eritrea, adjoining the Tigre highlands of Ethiopia, although the name Punt (perhaps Puwanet or Opunawet – ancient Egyptian writing does not represent vowels) seems to have survived into the Roman period in a place called Opone in Somalia near Cape Gardafui, which the Greeks called 'the Cape of Incense'. The magical land of Punt was, in short, a real place generally located in the region of the narrow straits between South Arabia and the Horn of Africa, and incense was among its most sought-after products. There are many other early accounts of this trade, all the way down to the sixth century BC, and it perhaps points us to a broad context for the biblical legend of the Queen of Sheba.

SAILING THE RED SEA IN THE ANCIENT WORLD

So how to travel to the mythical land? The ancient route between the Nile valley and Ethiopia and the Horn of Africa began with an overland journey to the Red Sea. This is also the route that later Ethiopian tradition says was taken by the Queen of Sheba on her way to and from Jerusalem, and it was the route I decided to follow. My old Baedeker guide for 1913 gives a list of the nightly stopping places from Coptos on the Nile, which were still used by caravans even at that time. Every one has ancient remains and inscriptions, Romans forts and wells; one roadside quarry has graffiti from the third millennium BC to the present day. We reached the sea at Quseir, about half-way down Egypt's Red Sea coast. This is a sleepy little

Opposite, top: An Egyptian embassy to Punt offers trade goods – raffia mats, tools, bronze axes and containers of wine. Below them is a band of water with fishes from the Red Sea.
Opposite, below: Raw incense is piled in heaps, ready to be transported back to Egypt along with incense trees which were planted outside Hatshepsut's temple.

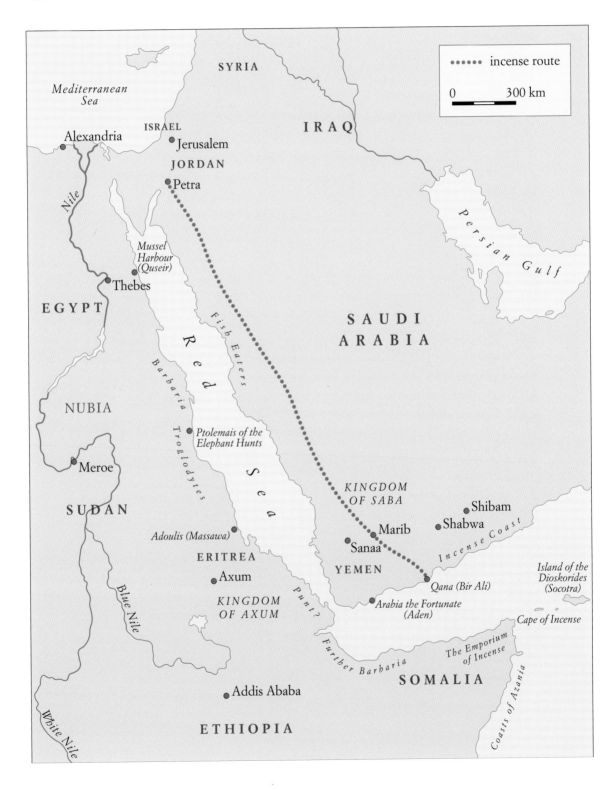

Mediterranean
Sea

SYRIA

IRAQ

Alexandria

ISRAEL
Jerusalem

JORDAN

Petra

Nile

Mussel
Harbour
(Quseir)

Thebes

EGYPT

Red Sea

Fish Eaters

Barbaria

Persian Gulf

SAUDI
ARABIA

NUBIA

Ptolemais of the
Elephant Hunts

Troglodytes

Meroe

SUDAN

Adoulis (Massawa)

ERITREA

Axum

KINGDOM
OF AXUM

Blue Nile

KINGDOM
OF SABA

Shibam

Marib

Shabwa

Sanaa

Incense Coast

YEMEN

Island of the
Dioskorides
(Socotra)

Punt?

Qana (Bir Ali)

Arabia the Fortunate
(Aden)

Cape of Incense

The Emporium
of Incense

Farther Barbaria

SOMALIA

Coasts of Azania

Addis Ababa

White Nile

ETHIOPIA

Opposite: The Red Sea, the Horn of Africa and Arabia at the time of the empires of Axum and Saba, with italicized place names from the Greek guidebook.
Above: Ancient graffiti on the road to the Red Sea.

medieval port with a crumbling incense barn and an Ottoman quarantine hospital for pilgrims travelling by sea from Mecca in Arabia. Close by, excavations by a British and Egyptian team have recently identified the port used in Greek times. It was then known as Muos Hormos, 'Mussel Harbour', and was the transhipment point for the East African, Arabian and Indian trades. Further up the coast at Mersa Gawesis, a promontory strewn with pottery marks the site of the port in Hatshepsut's time. This is where the Egyptians assembled their boats for the journey south, and where they returned with baboons and incense trees.

In ancient Egyptian times they would have sailed from dawn to dusk, covering perhaps 65 kilometres a day. Unfortunately, the Egyptians give no place names for the stopping places en route to the Horn of Africa. But later texts allow us to project back in time. A Greek merchant captain's *periplus*, or guidebook, gives us a detailed account of the Red Sea trade as far as the Persian Gulf and India, from the first century AD. Full of wonderful local details of ports and produce, sailing directions and weather patterns, it is one of the most fascinating books to have survived from the ancient world, and includes a description of the East African coast down to Tanzania. This text gives us our clues to relations between the Mediterranean, Arabia and Africa in ancient times, and leads us straight to the Ethiopian legend of the Queen of Sheba. So, with an ancient Greek merchant's guidebook in my rucksack, I set off from the sweltering Red Sea coast of Egypt hoping it would take me to the legendary kingdom of Sheba.

THE SEA JOURNEY TO ADOULIS

The dhow is gently rocking in a glassy harbour. The crew are asleep in the wheelhouse while the cook prepares breakfast in the tiny galley. Outside the heat of the day is coming on even though it has only just turned seven. In the previous few days we have made our way from Egypt through the Sudan, where we stayed at a little hotel run by a jovial Greek who still makes his summer trips to the Aegean in June and July, when the heat becomes unbearable. A man, I imagine, just like the Alexandrian Greek merchant of the *periplus* who recommends that 'The month of Tybi is the best time to make the sailing journey southwards down the Red Sea.' George calls his countrymen the 'Golden Greeks'. 'We've done it for thousands of years,' he laughs. 'You can still meet us in tavernas and bars across the Mediterranean and the Red Sea, waiting for the wind to change!'

The next stage of our journey is to sail on an old Red Sea dhow along the coast of Eritrea from Massawa to the site of the ancient Greek port of Adoulis.

Somnolent in the baking heat, Massawa is still shell-shocked from the war with Ethiopia. There are UN peacekeepers in the streets, and the palace of Haile Selassie is spattered with machine-gun holes. This beautiful old island, with its Ottoman merchants' houses, bazaars and warehouses, and the lovely yellow ochre tomb of an old Muslim saint, was once an important stopping place on the way to India, though now it feels left high and dry by history.

In the morning our dhow slowly rounds the headland of Massawa between the Dahlak islands and the African shore. We turn in southwards and the turquoise sea changes colour as we reach the shallows of an immense bay. We are heading for the site of the most famous port of Ethiopia in Greek and Roman times, which Ethiopian legend says was the main harbour of the Queen of Sheba's kingdom. From here, it is said, she departed for Jerusalem and returned bearing Solomon's son, Menelik.

Above: The journey by dhow to Adoulis on the Eritrean coast. For centuries such vessels plied the waters between the Persian Gulf, the Red Sea and India.

According to the *periplus*, in the first century AD the Greeks had a 'legally controlled emporium' on the Ethiopian coast called Adoulis. This was the main entrepôt for ivory, as well as a host of other goods, from the interior of Africa. The population included an expat Greek community which imported Italian wine and olive oil and often used Greek currency in its commerce. The wealth of the straits, combined with their strategic position, was naturally sought after. In recent times the British held Aden, in Yemen, and parts of the Horn of Africa. Back in the first century the Romans tried to do the same, sending expeditions down here to control the trade route. A recently discovered inscription from the islands between Djibouti and Yemen shows that a detachment of the Fourth Trajan Legion was billeted there as a permanent base for Roman trade with Arabia and the incense lands. These waters had long been well known to Egyptian and Mediterranean middlemen and the detailed description given by the Greek guidebook is still accurate today. Here is the approach to Adoulis:

Above: The lovely old Ottoman port on Massawa island. The anchorage has been used since ancient Egyptian times.
Opposite: The palace in Massawa was smashed in the recent war with Ethiopia.

> There is a deep bay extending due south, in front of which is an island called Oreine ['hilly'], which is about twenty miles from the innermost part of the bay and on both sides lies parallel to the coast. Here [i.e. at the island] at present arriving ships moor on the coast opposite the island. Two miles inland is the town of Adoulis. Further out is a large group of small islands, which are rich in tortoiseshell bartered from the local fisher people …

The ruins of the town have been found, just as the guidebook says, at the inner part of the bay. The island, with its hilly profile, can't be missed as you sail in from the north. Further out, the sandy islets of the Dahlak archipelago are still a rich source of tortoiseshell as the Greek author mentions. As for the former anchorage, what the Greeks called 'Diodoros island' is clearly Massawa island itself, which is just off the coast at the outermost edge of the bay and joined to the mainland by tidal flats, making it open to attacks by local Africans. This would also have been the ancient Egyptian landing place.

In the early centuries AD, Adoulis was a wealthy place. Local legend among today's fishing people on the coast says the ancient inhabitants lived a luxurious life with plentiful wine and fish. Today the ruins of their town lie on a low rise above a hot and desolate plain where camels graze in the scrub. The local villages – now with a mixture of corrugated-iron and raffia roofs – recall the *ichthyophagoi*, the 'Fish Eaters' in Greek texts. The town was built of volcanic stone, but embellished with imported marble whose fragments lie around us. A traveller in the 540s saw fine civic buildings and shrines, a monument to an Egyptian-Greek pharaoh, Ptolemy, and an inscription by Ezana, the Ethiopian King of Axum, recording his campaigns in the highlands of the Nile. Written in Greek, it bears testimony to the strange Hellenized world of an African kingdom in the days of the late Roman empire. The land was much more fertile then, and many have thought that this was what the ancient Egyptians knew as the land of Punt. It is certainly possible that incense was grown here in the past, though this no longer happens.

But all through history the island of Massawa, on the Eritrean coast, and the Bay of Adoulis were the gateway to the riches of the interior. The Greek *periplus* says it took eight days to travel overland to the metropolis of Axum itself, where 'all the ivory from beyond the Nile comes; the majority of elephant and rhino killed are from the upland region, though they are still to be seen in the coastal plain'. Two thousand years ago they had already been hunted there almost to extinction. Axum's main imports were Mediterranean linen, glass, brassware, copper armlets and anklets, and tools. And here in Adoulis, these clues from real historical sources bring us in touch with the legend. For what the ancient Greeks refer to as the metropolis of Axum, Ethiopian legend says was the Queen of Sheba's capital.

THE WOMAN WITH A GOAT'S FOOT

As we drove up the escarpment towards Asmara our Eritrean driver, Haile, told a story that is still known today by most members of the Ethiopian Orthodox Church: 'Once upon a time there was a rich Ethiopian merchant called Tamrin, who first visited Jerusalem carrying a cargo of gold and African hardwoods. When he told the queen what Solomon's kingdom was like, she wanted to go and see it for herself. And she took 797 loaded camels, countless mules and asses and she set out on her journey with her heart full of confidence in God.'

Haile also knows the legend of the queen herself, which is told in the Ethiopian Christians' sacred book, the Kebra Nagast, *The Glory of the Kings*: 'She was born deformed with one human foot and one hairy leg, like a goat, so she thinks she will never marry or have a lover.' In Jerusalem, Solomon has heard about her deformity and so arranges that to enter his palace she has to walk through a pool of water in which there is a piece of wood from the temple of Jerusalem.

'Solomon placed his throne by the side of the temple,' Haile continued, 'and he ordered his servants to flood the floor with water. When the Queen of Sheba saw this she hitched up her skirt so she could step across the water. Solomon glimpsed her legs and saw that the story was true. But when she touched the wood her deformed foot became like a human one.'

We will come across this strange tale again in Arabia. It appears in the Muslim holy book, the Koran, where Solomon's palace has a floor of glass or crystal, and the queen is both cured and converted to worship the true God. Written down in the seventh century AD, this may in fact be the ultimate source of the Ethiopian story.

Night was falling on our journey up from Massawa to the hill country of Eritrea. At the top of the escarpment we could see the hills of Ethiopia ahead, and the old road to Axum. Haile continued: 'So she stayed with Solomon and he made love to her – and to her woman too.' (He grinned. This story is depicted in pilgrims' pictures on vellum or paper, and on silk scarves, everywhere in Ethiopia today.)

'And then she returned and landed back here in Adoulis down on the coast, pregnant. She journeyed up this road to Axum and, according to Ethiopian

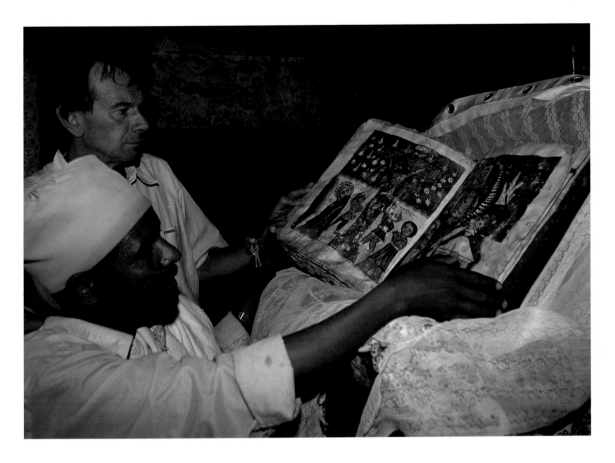

tradition, she gave birth to Menelik at Maribella close by here at Asmara. Then she returned to Axum, the capital of Ethiopia, where she ruled till she was old and where she was buried. And her son Menelik ruled after her.'

AXUM: A FORGOTTEN EMPIRE

Axum is a sleepy African provincial town today, but in Ethiopian legend it is famous as the capital of the Queen of Sheba. It's only 160 kilometres from Massawa as the crow flies, but the border has been closed by the liberation war that gave violent birth to the state of Eritrea. The road here from the Red Sea leads

Opposite: Debra Damo monastery on the route from the Red Sea to Axum. The only access to the monastery is by rope up a vertical cliff.
Above: Founded in the fifth century, the church possesses ancient books and even a hoard of Bactrian and Indo-Greek coins from Afghanistan.

across the wilds of Tigre through an extraordinary landscape of flat-topped mountains dotted with ancient monasteries. This was the route the ancient Greek merchants travelled with their crates of wine and bales of olives, as did the first Christian missionaries in the fourth century bearing the Bible story to the Greek-speaking kings of Axum.

Around the plain of Axum fabulous pinnacles rise up over the horizon, one a great spike of a peak like a brown Matterhorn, while all around us are crumbling brown fields hedged with drystone walls. In parched ravines are waving clumps of eucalyptus and the faintest residue of green grass where cattle gather. The rains are expected soon. It is easy to see how devastating it can be here when they don't come and the crops fail. In modern times this has been a land of famine compounded by corrupt and murderous regimes colluded with by the West. Bitter civil war and liberation struggle have left the place on its knees; but now at last there is cause for optimism. Ethiopia is dancing again, and here in Tigre one of the hopes for the future lies in the extraordinary riches of the past.

The town of Axum is low-rise, with a straggle of bars and tiny hotels, mud walls painted in yellow ochre and bright blue. A huge plane tree in the central square gives shade to the crowds that gather for the Saturday market. Tethering their camels and donkeys, women sell cloths and brightly coloured baskets. But the visitor soon notices that the modern town rises from the debris of a much more ancient time, for this is a vast archaeological ruin field. In the little park by the soft-drinks stand are columns, and column bases, and a huge stela with an inscription in Greek. (The *periplus* mentions that the local rulers here used Greek and that one, indeed, spoke it 'excellently'.) Everywhere there are fragments of monumental sculpture. Especially the square-grooved bases of one of the typical Axumite monuments – oversized stone thrones that were once erected with inscriptions commemorating the Axumite kings. Elaborate underground royal tombs in excellent, squared masonry are dotted around the town, one of them behind the police station. Sadly, however, the foundations of the huge royal residence, known locally as the Queen of Sheba's palace, were almost totally destroyed by road building during the Italian occupation in the 1930s.

The most striking of Axum's ancient monuments, though, are the stelas. Apparently royal memorials, over 120 stelas survive, in whole or part, in the town and fields. Some are broken and some have fallen, and one huge specimen was

Opposite: Market day in Axum, Ethiopia. Today's inhabitants live among the spectacular ruins of what the Romans called 'the metropolis of the Axumites'.

taken to Italy in the 1930s, though it is soon to return. Others still stand over 20 metres high, and one fallen monster measures 33 metres and weighs in at well over 500 tonnes. As far as we know, it is the largest stela ever made.

Among the ancient civilizations rediscovered in modern times, Axum was perhaps the last to register in the Western consciousness. The myth of its immense antiquity is laid out in the sacred scriptures of the Ethiopian Church, and appears unchallenged in today's tourist guidebooks:

> Since 4370 BC Aksum was the seat of the Ethiopian kings …
> this civilization was particularly dynamic during the reign of the
> Queen of Sheba, due to foreign trade relations, administration, religion
> and other social institutions. The Queen of Sheba also entered into
> good diplomatic relations with the biblical King Solomon in about

1000 BC. Until the birth of Christ, 62 kings from the Agazian tribe reigned after her … and a total of 255 kings back to 4370 BC, before the earliest Pharaohs.

The more prosaic reality is still fascinating; but, curiously, as far as the archaeologists can tell, Axum in fact has no deep roots in time at all. For Axum only begins at the start of the first century AD, long after the time in which a real-life Queen of Sheba could have lived. Axum is in fact the product of the dramatic opening up of the world after the age of Alexander the Great. In what we call the Hellenistic age (from 300 BC to the first century AD) Greek culture became internationalized, and mixed with Jewish, Egyptian, Indian and Persian influences.

Like today's Americans, the Greeks created an international civilization, and many local cultures aped it, from Afghanistan to the Horn of Africa, coveting their brilliant advances in technology, art and politics. On the fringe of this immense zone of Hellenized culture lay the Axum region, controlling a key trade route into the heart of Africa. The town of Axum rose swiftly to be the centre of a powerful kingdom, with fine temples, tombs and palaces. In the late first century AD the city was already a 'metropolis of Africa' (or at least the Africa the Greeks knew). By the third century its fame had spread to Persia, and in the fourth its rulers adopted Christianity through Greek-speaking missionaries from Syria and Egypt. This took place around 330, at the same time that the emperor Constantine declared the Roman empire Christian. Ethiopia, in fact, may just be the earliest Christian country in the world.

Because of its role in the conversion, from that day to this Axum has remained the most important centre of the Ethiopian Orthodox Church. There were periods during the fourth and sixth centuries AD when the Christian African kings of Axum ruled parts of the Red Sea coast of Arabia and Yemen. But with the rise of Islam their power declined, although an eighth-century painting from Jordan curiously shows the King of Axum still rubbing shoulders with the Byzantine emperor and the Shah of Persia.

It was in 1270 that the revived medieval kingdom of Ethiopia introduced, as an explicit part of its official ideology, the idea that its dynasty was descended from the Queen of Sheba and her son by Solomon, Menelik. However, Axum never again exerted political power, and the locals lived amid its ruins, keeping up their ancient churches, until Western travellers, fascinated by its legends and ancient remains, began visiting from the sixteenth century onwards. Archaeologists first explored the ruins a century ago. Photographs taken by the German expedition in

1906 show Axum as a village of circular, thatched huts where a few thousand people lived in the shadow of the astonishing monuments of their ancestors: the great stelas and the mother church of Ethiopian Christianity with its associated chapel of the Ark of the Covenant which, according to the Kebra Nagast, the Ethiopian Book of Kings, was brought back by Menelik from Jerusalem.

Above: Stelas at Axum – monuments to the rulers of this African empire between the first and fourth centuries AD. One is thought to be the largest obelisk ever carved.

THE QUEEN OF SHEBA AND THE LOST ARK

Tonight in Axum is the 'Night of Mary', and the sacred precinct is full of people and lights; the sound of drums and chanting rises in the night to the hilltop hotel where we are staying. Down below among the trees women are dancing in their white cotton robes around a cluster of ancient pillars half-buried in the ground; to one side is a great jumbled heap of ancient throne bases before which the kings of old must have performed their rituals. Inside the precinct, pilgrims gather at the fence of the ark shrine to receive holy water from the guardian who lives permanently inside the little enclosure, which he may never leave. From the big church the sound of singing and drumming echoes all night.

The main church (which only men may enter) is a splendid barn of a place. This was the coronation site of the Ethiopian kings right down to Haile Selassie, Ras Tafari, in the 1930s. According to tradition, it was founded in around 340 in the reign of the Kings Abraha and Asbeha. Numismatic and inscriptional evidence

Opposite: An Ethiopian pilgrim at Axum.
Above: The shrine of the Ark of the Covenant (left) and the great basilica of the Church of Mary Zion, the mother church of Ethiopia (right).

singles out Abraha, or Ezana as he is also called, and suggests the date is roughly right. The basilica stands in a raised oval enclosure that must presumably be the site of the pre-Christian Axumite kings' sanctuary. It is about 90 by 120 metres in size with a smaller raised inner precinct – perhaps 35 by 45 metres – which is literally strewn with fragments of ancient pillars, corbels, column bases, shafts and finely carved capitals. The interior is bright yellow and the walls are covered with garish murals. Splendidly cloaked priests with long beards and tall hats perform the all-night vigil. Their rituals are close to those of the Coptic Church, and hence distantly to the ancient Egyptians too, especially when they shake the sistra (rattles) to the booming of enormous African drums.

Several Greek inscriptions have been found here. Twenty years ago, by the path leading up to one of the main royal tombs, farmers discovered a big stela bearing the name of Ezana himself, who is called 'King of Axum and of the Ethiopians'. The use of the word 'Ethiopian' in earlier Greek texts, it is perhaps worth pointing out, means simply 'black-skinned people', hence Africans in general. In the *Odyssey*, composed in *c.* 700 BC, they are 'the most remote of men'. A narrower definition appears in the work of the historian Herodotus in the fifth century BC. He refers to the lands of Egypt south of Elephantine as being Ethiopia, and to Meroe in Sudan as 'the capital of Ethiopia'. Similarly, in the New Testament (Acts 8:27) there is a reference to the homeland of a 'eunuch of Ethiopia', who was baptized by Jesus on the road between Gaza and Jerusalem. He is the treasurer to a ruler called Candake (who we know from inscriptional evidence was actually a ruler in Meroe in Sudan). The name Candake was another of the names subsequently attached to the Queen of Sheba; at roughly the same time the Roman Jewish writer Josephus called her an Ethiopian. But in the Axum inscriptions we begin to see the narrowing down of the meaning of Ethiopia to describe the area covered by the medieval and modern state. A state in which the Queen of Sheba was the indisputable founder of the royal line, even though as we now know she could never have ruled from Axum. So where, then, was the Iron Age predecessor of the city known to the Greeks?

CHRISTIANS, ETHIOPIANS AND SABAEANS

We are back at the hotel now, and the heat of the day is fading as the sun sets over the surrounding bowl of hills. The sound of chanting is still coming from the church; hawks circle overhead, and local women are washing clothes at the big tank known as Sheba's Bath. At the great stela below us a wedding party arrives, and the bride kisses the stela's foot before posing for her photo, her white dress billowing in the warm evening wind. Around the dining-room walls are twenty panels painted on vellum which tell the legendary version of the tale: the Queen of Sheba sailing past the pyramids, making love to Solomon and giving birth to Menelik. In front of me on the table are photographs and maps from the German expedition of 1906. The photos show archaeologists sifting through fragments when many more remains, now lost, were visible above ground. As I pull out my notebook to scribble these notes, I am still wondering how to make sense of the Ethiopian story. If Axum only comes into existence in the first century AD, is the whole Ethiopian version of the Queen of Sheba story a pure fiction? Where did the Ethiopian legend come from?

Clues to the origin of the pre-Axumite culture of Ethiopia are there to see, recorded a century ago in the notes and photos of the German expedition. A kilometre or two away from us, hidden in the rocky hills behind our hotel, is a little shrine dedicated to St Pantaleon, a Byzantine-Greek monk who built a church here in either the fifth or sixth century AD. This tiny place is where one Axumite Christian king, Kaleb, is said to have become a hermit after renouncing the crown. It's a beautiful spot, on top of a rocky hill which you ascend by nearly a hundred steps cut into the rock, the last few made of reused, ancient stone slabs. The sacred precinct is a circle only about 18 metres across, and the church itself is tiny, maybe 12 metres long. You can't see it so clearly now, because the church was rebuilt recently and most of the clues were destroyed, but in 1906 the Germans photographed a building made out of bits of an older shrine, incorporating fragments of columns, a granite bowl and a small slab from a stela. A Greek inscription was built into the east front, and there was another in honour of the god of war Ares, or Mahrem in the native language. The Germans had found the unmistakable remains of an ancient Christian shrine and an even earlier pagan temple. And here's the surprise: the temple also had a beautifully written inscription in Sabaean script, the script of Iron Age South Arabia, the historical kingdom of Saba – which many scholars believe is the real kingdom behind the biblical land of Sheba.

More recently, in the 1950s, Ethiopian archaeologists investigated a mysterious site 15 kilometres away from Axum at Hawelti. This was a low, dome-shaped hill rising above fertile fields that marked the site of a big city where square-sectioned monoliths, strangely resembling those found in the temples of Iron Age Arabia, still stick out of the ground. They discovered high quality sculpture, including a limestone throne with finely carved reliefs and an ibex-head frieze of a kind that is known only from early Arabia. In the prehistory of the kingdom of

Axum the signs were beginning to suggest strongly that South Arabia was the catalyst for the first urban civilization of Ethiopia. Clinching evidence for this connection lies at another site on the road from Axum to the Red Sea, in one of the most extraordinary and mysterious monuments in Africa.

THE MYSTERY OF YEHA

We are heading back up the road from Axum to the Red Sea. This has become a frontier zone since the bitter battles in Tigre with the Eritreans, and the bars in the roadside halts are full of young soldiers. At the turn-off we follow a dirt track for several kilometres through wild, arid and eroded hills. It is easy to imagine human origins in this landscape, which is primordial in the real sense of the word. The land is parched. However, the village of Yeha has water, and just before you reach it you enter a fertile green oasis of wheat fields, great stands of eucalyptus, and meadows still with a faint covering of grass where the animals graze along a dried-up water-course. Soon you turn into a little dusty square, where children are playing football. At the far side the sacred enclosure rises in front of you above the trees and gardens. A flight of stone steps leads up to the little hill surrounded by a great circular, drystone wall. Passing through the gate you come to another set of steps which leads to a second circle inside the first. This is the ancient sacred precinct, and inside, among the trees, there are two churches surrounded by a graveyard. The main one has a grand stairway leading to its door. Over to the right is a huge stone structure, a giant, barn-like building roughly 18 metres square with towering walls, over 10 metres high, constructed from skilfully joined masonry. It is empty now, but in the far corner of the interior are the remains of a baptistry. Like Axum and the shrine of St Pantaleon, this was an ancient structure later converted into a Christian church.

We learn more from the account of a Portuguese missionary who came here in 1521. Inside the enclosure Francisco Alvarez saw 'a fine church of the Virgin Mary, and next to it a mighty tower and stately houses'. Locals told him that the ancient 'tower' belonged to the biblical queen, Kandake, Queen of Sheba. Another tale, another name: a protean woman.

The tower had in fact been a temple. A frieze of ibex heads built into the front of the modern church was part of an ancient frieze that once ran round the temple's interior, and is identical to the fragment found at Hawelti, near Axum.

Opposite: The remains of the mysterious temple at Yeha, dating perhaps from the sixth century BC, though epigraphical evidence may put it even earlier.

What is even more tantalizing is that it is identical to the frieze discovered at the great seventh-century BC temple of the Moon God in Marib, in the heart of Yemen in South Arabia. Royal tombs have been discovered in the side of the hill at Yeha, and female statues, perhaps of deities. On another low hill, 200 metres away, another structure has massive square-sectioned monolithic pillars of a type known from Arabia and also found in Ethiopia at Hawelti. Most intriguingly, inscribed stones, carved in the Sabaean script of South Arabia, have also been discovered which are now locked up under fine red cloths in a side chapel. This same script was found in the little chapel of St Pantaleon. The clues all begin to point in the same direction.

Yeha was probably the ancient city of Ava, capital of the kingdom of Damat between the eighth and fifth centuries BC. It covered 8 hectares and had a population of perhaps ten thousand who spoke a language that was Semitic (as is the Geez language of northern Ethiopia still spoken today). Its honorifics (e.g. 'mkrb' meaning 'ruler' or 'bringer of unity', and 'mlk' meaning 'king') are the same in ancient Sabaean and modern Arabic. It is the only civilization with monumental architecture, writing and sculpture so far found in Ethiopia to take us back before the middle of the first millennium BC.

Frustratingly little is yet known of Yeha and its mysterious monuments. But clearly a pre-Axumite civilization is waiting to be discovered, one that at some point during the period after 500 BC was closely connected to, and strongly influenced by, the kingdom of Saba in South Arabia. What then was the relation between this culture and Yemeni culture? Did the kings (and queens) of Saba rule here in the middle of the first millennium BC? And was this the pathway for the legend of the Queen of Sheba? The next phase of our journey now led us across the straits into Yemen to see for ourselves the enigmatic monuments of Saba.

YEMEN: ARABIA THE FORTUNATE

Dawn at Bir Ali, on the Arabian Sea. A pale blue light and a calm sea. We are sleeping on the beach where Freya Stark landed in 1935 to be greeted by tribesmen in loincloths with curved Yemeni daggers. These days they have Kalashnikovs. On the soft white sand there is a tide of delicate coral stems, scarlet and orange, and

Opposite: In Yemen, the traditional heartland of Arabia.
Overleaf: Fishing boats near Bir Ali on the Incense Coast by the Arabian Sea.

pink spondylus shells. Behind the beach a scrubby plain stretches across to undulating sills of black lava seamed with wind-blown sand; further inland, jagged black mountains disappear into the haze. The heat of the day will soon be on us.

At the north end of the beach stands a craggy black promontory called Crow Rock, in the lee of which are terraces of black squared masonry, the remains of a temple and an agora. On the other side is a wide bay where scores of blue fishing boats ride the gentle swell. This is the ancient anchorage of Qana, to which the *periplus* says 'all the incense of Arabia is brought by camels and skin rafts, and from where trade goes as far as Africa, India, Oman and Persia'. This forgotten beach was the beginning of the frankincense road that led north to Petra, Damascus, Jerusalem and the Mediterranean, once one of the earliest and richest long-distance trade routes in the world. Right up to the 1930s about 1200 tons of frankincense a year came through the ports of Yemen and Dufar, wafting 'Sabaean odours from the spicy shore of Araby the Blest', as Milton puts it. As always the *periplus* is spot on with its local detail; just as it says, there is a rocky islet immediately offshore. This is Bird Island, and a bigger island lies several kilometres out. I rest the book on my rucksack and take some coarse bread and black tea. We are about to leave the beach and head off into the interior of South Arabia on the ancient trail of the incense caravans to Saba.

I like the old captain who wrote the Greek guide in around AD 70. I imagine he must have been old in order to have had such an intimate knowledge of so many landing places, harbours and peoples. No doubt he would have agreed with the author of the *Odyssey* – a book he surely knew – that there are few better things in life than to 'travel far and wide, see the cities of many peoples and learn their ways'.

The Incense Coast, for which Qana is the main port, occupies a wonderful position between the Red Sea, the Persian Gulf, the Horn of Africa and India. The Romans called it Arabia Felix – 'Fortunate Arabia', a land lucky in its position in the world, its climate and its natural produce. Civilization here was deep-rooted and had a magnificent flowering in the first millennium BC. In later periods Greek influence was strong in Arabia, and the Romans coveted its wealth. In 24 BC Aulus Gallus even invaded Saba by land. Its wealth lasted till the time of the Prophet, when Islam, the religion of desert Arabia, burst from the peninsula to change the world. Its land routes, though, go back well before 800 BC, when regular contacts with the Near East were established. From then the states of South Arabia, including the historical kingdom of Saba, grew wealthy on this trade.

And here perhaps is the closest context for the Bible story: real primary historical records exist here, which immediately enable us to enter a more solid

world than that created by Ethiopian legend. In their monumental inscriptions the Assyrian kings, in what is now Iraq, begin to make tantalizing references soon after 800 BC to embassies from Arabia, sometimes led or sent by queens. In the 730s and 720s we find a reference to a 'tribute from Shamsi, Queen of Arabia and Itamar the Sabaean'. The rule of Shamsi was a long one, over twenty years, and she was evidently a redoubtable character who was prepared to come to blows with the overweening powers of Assyria. Other queens included Shamsi's successor Iatie, in around 700 BC and one Telkhunu. All these 'rulers of the seashore and of the desert', according to one Assyrian king, ruled 'countries far away to the west who heard the fame of my rule and brought to me all kinds of spices'. Interestingly,

Above: The valley of Petra in Jordan. A great trading city on the route from Arabia to Jerusalem, Petra levied its tolls on the incense caravans that came through from Saba in South Arabia.

among them Shamsi is listed as a tributary along with Hiram, King of Tyre (a contemporary of Solomon in the Bible). The Assyrians never actually ruled faraway Saba, but in their fashion they interpreted such missions as a kind of submission. Though none of the queens who is named is likely to have been from Saba, these texts show that there really were independent queens in Arabia in biblical times, queens who sent, and even led, embassies to the Near East, bearing incense and other treasures as gifts. Here then at last is a plausible context for the Bible story: Near Eastern diplomacy and gift-giving of the eighth and seventh centuries BC and the kingdom of Saba, with its main centre at Marib. And Marib was to be the goal of the last leg of our journey.

THE LAND OF SAND

Amid the sandstorms on the wilder stretches of the coast road on our way towards Mukalla, we glimpse flimsy settlements with the same thatched huts and beached canoes we saw on the Eritrean shore, and which you can see all the way across to the Makran coast of Pakistan. They belong to the modern descendants of the primitive people known to the ancients as the *ichthyophagoi*, the 'Fish Eaters', still hanging on in defiance of the modern state and its ways. In the middle of the day, in torrid heat, we leave the coast road and turn north up to the high plateau of Arabia, which stretches all the way across the Empty Quarter to the Holy Land. The surface area of the Arabian Peninsula as far as the Syrian Desert is larger, astonishingly, than western Europe or India, and it is mostly sand. No wonder civilization has been tenacious in those areas where nature and climate have combined to make it delightful, if still a little hot, to live.

The Hadramaut, in the Koranic 'Land of Sand', lies four hours' drive north of Mukalla, over the high desert. It is burning hot and you drive through a permanent shimmering white haze. In the late afternoon we come down into the wadi to see a spellbinding vision of fertility in the midst of a waterless wilderness. This is the biggest, most fertile wadi in the Arabian Peninsula and sustains a magical series of ancient towns, which appear one after another like oases, tucked under the cliffs of the wadi, or out in the valley bottom surrounded by bright green fields and waving palm forests.

In the evening we reach Shibam, a giant cube of whitewashed buildings rising above emerald-green palm groves like an ancient Babylonian city, or, as the Shibamites like to call it, a Manhattan of the desert. In front of the town there is a mud-brick defence wall, and rising above this, medieval high-rises – ten, twelve

and even thirteen storeys tall. The houses are also built of brown, mud bricks and they are crowned with painted plaster crenellations, and great bands of whitewash, with picturesque crumbling little minarets poking up between them. We lodge for the night under the eastern wall at a nice 1930s hotel with a fine old garden full of songbirds.

Here we meet an old Islamic scholar who sings us the Koranic verses about the Queen of Sheba, and gives us the orthodox interpretation of the tale as told in the Koran: 'the Queen of the South' who visited Solomon. There was, he said, no doubt in Islamic tradition that she was a queen not in Africa but in Arabia, and that

Above: At the Great Mosque in Shibam. 'There are few more delightful places in the world,' wrote a tenth-century Persian geographer.

she appears also in Muslim and Christian texts as the Queen of the South. Her kingdom, which we call Sheba, he said, was Saba in Yemen. And again the same strange story of the goat's leg:

> She was bidden to enter the palace and when she saw it she thought there was a pool of water and bared her legs. But Solomon said, 'It is a palace paved with glass.' 'Lord,' she replied. 'I have sinned against my own soul. Now I bow with Solomon to Allah, Lord of Creation.'
> Koran, Sura 27

So in the Koran the woman of power, the sun worshipper, with a hairy foot like a goat, is cured by the miraculous wooden beam and turns to the true God. Some Jewish and Islamic traditions interpret this by associating her with demonic spirits, djinns, and in particular with the ancient Babylonian and Semitic demoness, Lilith. Modern critics have thought the tale came from a folk story demonizing women in a patriarchal tradition.

'So should we understand this as a symbolic narrative,' I asked the scholar, 'or does the Muslim tradition interpret it literally?'

'Literally,' he answered. 'People can be born deformed in this way. I believe it is best understood literally.'

This strange tale, which we had first heard from our driver in Ethiopia, spread across much of the world. It was recycled in the Christian West, probably after the crusaders heard it in the Holy Land, and you will even find the woman with the goat's foot depicted on medieval prayer stalls in England and on cathedral mosaics in Italy. But the story first found in the Koran is perhaps the source of the Ethiopian tale, and maybe of all later versions. It survives in many versions from as far away as Turkey, Persia and northern India, all of which include the strange detail of the queen walking over water or glass at the threshold of the palace or temple. Similar kinds of tale, demonizing women of power, are found in many cultures across the world, especially in monotheistic ones. One might guess, however, that the origins of this, the most widespread version, lie in pre-Islamic Arabian folk story. How such a tale might have arisen we will come to in due course.

Opposite and overleaf: Shibam – a still-living medieval caravan city in the Wadi Hadramaut. A Manhattan of the desert, Shibam's mud-brick houses were increased in height over many generations as their owners' families grew in size.

The next stage of our journey was to follow the Incense Road north from Shibam and then west across the edge of the Empty Quarter to Marib. It is an area till recently out of government control, so a Bedouin guide came with us in a four-wheel-drive pick-up (few Bedu use camels these days). After climbing one big belt of dunes, we settled down to a steady pace across hard, flat, scrubby desert, empty but for a few lone camels that chewed impassively as we shot past. At dusk we arrived at the mound of Shabwa, the ancient capital of the Hadramaut, and drove on to the sandy slopes within its outer walls and pitched camp. We spent the night stretched out under cotton sheets till at four o'clock a cool breeze heralded the first light. Around us we began to make out immense mud-brick walls and bastions rendered almost shapeless now by wind and rain. Deserted only about forty years ago, this was the ancient caravan city of Shabwa.

A LOST CIVILIZATION OF ARABIA

> There was a sign for Sheba in olden days, a sign in their homeland –
> two gardens one on the right hand, one on the left: 'Eat of the
> sustenance provided by your Lord, and be grateful to Him: a territory
> beautiful and happy.'
> Koran, Sura 34

Dawn over Shabwa. We breakfast on black tea, flat bread and eggs, and then walk up to the city ruins. There were once sixty temples, according to the Greek geographer Strabo. With its 8-kilometre wall and even larger outer circuit, Shabwa gives a vivid sense of the size and wealth of these ancient South Arabian cities. In scale, it reminds me of some of the giant city mounds of southern Iraq: strewn with a deep tide of broken pottery, bits of wood, rope and tattered textiles left by the last inhabitants. In the years since it was deserted its crumbling towers have turned to melted mud, running away down the gullies in dried rivulets. In the centre, where the biggest shrine stood, there is now a vast, gouged-out hole. The main city god here was Saween, to whom all caravan managers who came through had to dedicate a portion of their wealth as a toll. 'Its citizens were drowsy with the scent of incense, with so many caravans coming through,' wrote one classical writer. 'So they had to smoke other substances simply in order to keep awake!'

Opposite: Rising to heights of 30 or 40 metres, many of Shibam's houses are five hundred years old.

The next day we set off on the second part of our desert crossing. On the final leg of our journey we were to cross from the ancient kingdom of the Hadramaut into the territory of Marib, the historical Saba – a name that Arabs believe is the most likely source of the biblical Sheba.

After a few hours' driving over flat, hard desert we finally hit the blistering tarmac road to Saudi Arabia in the early afternoon; all around us was an oppressive heat haze, brown earth blending into brown sky. At a truck stop we saw half a dozen long-distance coaches plying between Saudi and Oman. In the shade a crowd of people – truck drivers, pilgrims, travellers – gathered round as dealers unwrapped bundles of fresh green *qat*, the mildly narcotic leaf chewed by everyone in the Horn of Africa and South Arabia as digestive, relaxant, aphrodisiac and hallucinogen. Finally we were on the last stretch. After a couple of hours we came out of the dreary, monochrome desert of sand, and entered a fertile land in a bowl of green hills. We had reached Marib, the heartland of the ancient kingdom of Saba.

Following centuries of poverty and isolation, Marib's modern fertility was created by a new dam built in the 1960s, but this was preceded back in the first millennium BC by a great dam higher up the valley a few kilometres out of town. This was part of a remarkable system of dams, canals and wells that turned ancient Marib into a fabled garden of plenty that was remembered for centuries in the Bible and the literature of the Near East, Arabia and even ancient Greece.

The great dam is the most impressive stonework of ancient Arabia. It was designed to catch water run-offs and flash floods from the high plateau during the monsoon season, which lasted from April till summer. It is an astonishing archaeological survival. A few facts will help to convey its scale. The towering southern anchor of squared masonry rears like a fortress wall, 18 metres high with its bastions and a giant sluice gate. The dam itself stretched across a gap of about 700 metres, it was 55 metres thick at its base and in its middle the water reached a depth of 15 metres. It irrigated 100 square kilometres of farmland and sustained a city population of between 30,000 and 50,000. The agricultural wealth of Saba was founded on this dam, which was built in the eighth century BC when the kingdom was rising to power and fame, enabling it to rule for periods across the Red Sea in the Yeha region of Ethiopia. Repaired many times, the dam finally broke in about AD 575, around the time of the Prophet Muhammad's birth. The Prophet came from a merchant family that plied the route up into Palestine and Syria; his first

---

Opposite: The huge sluice gate at the great dam at Marib. Built in the eighth century BC, the dam was finally broken in the late sixth century AD.

wife was the widow of a caravan master, and she managed the family business after her first husband's death; both she and the Prophet would have known the route down to Marib. The story of the breaking of the dam is mentioned in the Koran: how the two wonderful gardens of the land of Saba, one on the right-hand side and one on the left, were destroyed by flooding in an act of God. With that the wealth of the ancient kingdom was gone. Without the dam and its irrigation system, the city declined and spent the Middle Ages as a fortified mud-brick town with a few score towered houses, its people sustained by wells in a parched plain – until in the late twentieth century they went back to the ancient blueprint.

THE KINGDOM OF SABA

> I have seen a land ruled by a Queen who worships the sun.
> She possesses a magnificent throne and is provided with everything
> one could desire.
> *Koran*, Sura 17

Saba was the greatest kingdom of South Arabia. The oasis has a huge number of ancient villages, sanctuaries, cemeteries and irrigation systems. The first settlements appear soon after 2000 BC. In about 1200 BC a local kingdom was created with a distinctive culture, and in the eighth and seventh centuries a remarkable flowering is attested to by hundreds of inscriptions. This was the state known to the Assyrian kings and their diplomats, and to the authors of the Old Testament. The great dam was part of a building programme of extraordinary monuments from the eighth century BC, which also point to a powerful regional state existing here. If we can identify the biblical Sheba with this state, then we can begin to narrow down the source of the legend and paint a picture of the real kingdom that lies behind the tale.

Excavations in Marib in the last few decades have uncovered a hitherto unknown lost civilization from the eighth century BC. Traces of four great temples have emerged from the desert. One is the Awwan temple, dedicated to the Moon God, Almaqah, the national god of the Sabaeans. (The sun, the moon and the morning star were central to the ancient cults of Marib, as was remembered long afterwards in the Koran.) It was clearly an important place for the royal rituals of the Sabaean state. It is oval in shape and lies in a great circular enclosure with finely jointed walls that still stand nearly 10 metres high. In some ways the temple resembles the one in Yeha in Ethiopia. It has an axis over 90 metres long with eight dramatic monoliths erected in a line 9 metres from its entrance and standing about 12 metres high. Completely covered in sand until the 1950s, it has been damaged and plundered in the civil wars since the 1960s, but it is now again under excavation and consolidation. An extraordinary feature of the temple is that there is only one entrance to the oval enclosure, through a columned hall 18 metres square. The doorway contained a large bronze basin full of water fed by an underground spring, and the rulers and their priests had to walk through it in order to enter the inner enclosure. In all Marib shrines, in fact, there seems to have been a close connection between water ablutions and purifying rites, and the worship of the Moon God or Moon Goddess. Dare one see here an uncanny echo of the Koranic, Ethiopian and later medieval legends of the queen stepping over flowing water, or glass, at the threshold of a palace or temple? Could this be coincidence? Or could the Koranic tale have preserved an oral South Arabian tradition from before the Islamic era?

Much better preserved is the Bar'an temple nearly a mile away to the north. It is set by a spring in a delightful grove of palms, with neat mud-brick farmhouses in the field next door; water is still plentiful here and the fields are very fertile. Also known as 'the throne of Balquis [the Queen of Sheba]', it too was dedicated to Almaqah, the Lord of the Moon and the Lord of Ibexes, and has been beautifully excavated and conserved in recent years by German archaeologists. All the details are clear and can still be read today. It is square in shape. There was a sacred well in the middle of the enclosure with a pool supplied with water by a channel from the mouth of a bull. The cult basins have ibex-headed waterspouts, and incense burners from the site bear sun and horned-moon emblems. A flight of steps leads up to the inner chamber, which stood behind six huge monoliths with carved tops and decorated crowns, each one 12 metres in height. In the sanctum some of the altars are still in their places, giving a vivid impression of the long-dead Sabaean royal cult. As the wind stirs the palms and the pumps in the fields chug away, one can almost smell the incense smoke; and the perfumed presence of the kings and queens of Saba is almost tangible.

The temple was initially built in the late second and early first millennium BC, and a second phase started in the eighth century BC, when all of Marib grew in prosperity. During this period Saba and its neighbour Ophir became well known

Overleaf: The temple of Bar'an in Marib, one of three known temples of the capital of the Sabaeans. The temple was rebuilt in the eighth century BC, around the time when a historical Queen of Sheba might have lived. The dramatic and rather modernist monoliths are typical of the South Arabian style.

to the powers of the Near East. As we have already seen, this was the time when the Assyrians recorded the names of several Arabian queens – Shamsi, Zabibe and Iatie. These queens led caravans to the Near East and Syria, one of which was robbed on the Syrian Euphrates. It would be tantalizing if one of them actually were the queen in the Bible, but it is more likely that the Assyrian records refer to north Arabians. However, the general evidence – that queens led embassies to the Near East and Assyria from the Arabian Peninsula, followed by caravans bearing incense and spices – fits perfectly with the Bible story. This, I tend to think, was the 'historical kernel' at the beginning of the fairy story.

And the sequel? Inscriptions show that the ancient gods of sun and moon were still worshipped in Marib in the Roman period. In the fourth century AD, though, one of the local kings adopted Christianity, and the Sabaean gods were incorporated into the new pantheons and began to fade away. With the triumph of Islam in the seventh century AD this old world of Arabia went for ever. In the Koran and later Islamic traditions the Sabaeans and their queen are remembered as sun worshippers who learned the error of their ways. But the magical civilization of Saba cast a long shadow. Even now, in the very heart of Islam at Mecca itself, during the festival of the Haj, as millions of pilgrims from around the world circle around the ancient sacred black stone of the Kaaba, they are preserving something of the old customs of pre-Islamic Arabia, a distant living link with the days of the Queen of Sheba and the ancient civilization that underlies their modern world.

THE CITY OF SHEBA

> Here she lived for ninety years, subduing the lands
> from distant Iraq to the edge of the great sand
> a thousand thousands to obey her commands
> ABD-KARIB AS'AD, KING OF SABA *Ode to the Queen of Sheba c.* AD 400

So, finally, where did the queen live? The last clue is easy to miss. If you drive out of Marib towards the north, past the ribbon of truck stops, roadside cafés and long-distance hostels, you soon see a huge mound rising up with pinnacles of ruined mud-brick towers. This is old Marib, the remains of what was once the citadel mound of the ancient kingdom of Saba. Here, if anywhere, stood the palaces of the rulers of Saba in the Iron Age and later. An outer wall of mud brick, now vanished, sheltered the main urban population of at least 30,000, maybe nearer twice that. Approaching through the fields you see the line of the inner walls of the town enclosing undulating heaps of ruins. This circuit of about 3 kilometres contained stone temples and the houses of nobles, functionaries, merchants and the lesser royal kin. You pass the footings of a stone gate by the side of the modern road; the gates led out to temples in the north and the northeast – the great 'national' shrines to the gods of the sun and moon, which were situated in idyllic spots out in the fields and linked by festal paths for the royal ceremonies.

The central mound still has a dramatic skyline of half-ruined mud-brick Yemeni tower houses. People are still living in them, and a battered pick-up comes to a halt, bringing jerrycans of water from a well in the fields while children play with kites. Coming up on to the lower part of the mound, the first thing you see is a ruined Ottoman fortress with circular towers, its stone perimeter walls cracked and overgrown – it was bombed in air attacks during the civil war. Made of reused masonry, the fortress walls are studded with ancient inscriptions. Following the track up on to the higher part of the mound, you reach a derelict water tower built out of ancient stonework; and there behind a cluster of trees, amid heaps of debris and broken columns, you notice an abandoned mosque. At first sight you might pass it by without a second glance, but a closer look reveals that it is entirely constructed from the remains of ancient buildings. The prayer hall, once roofed in rough wooden branches and plastered over, has now partly fallen in. But it still has twenty or so standing columns that clearly once belonged to an older Sabaean palatial or religious building. More broken columns and architectural fragments are lying in heaps outside, and the steps and retaining walls of the mosque are made from huge old stones. But the greatest source of astonishment in this sad picture of dereliction are eight huge, standing monoliths, just like the ones in the Awwan temple. Behind them lie more stone buildings made from ancient rubble, and a massive well at least 15 metres deep. In this place ablutions and rituals must have been performed by the kings of Saba (and no doubt the queens too).

Here, then, on the edge of the citadel mound of old Marib itself were the remains of a great Sabaean temple from the first millennium BC. Probably it survived as a structure right through to the Islamic conquest, and at some later point was converted into a mosque. Some thirty years ago, during the civil war, it was due to be demolished, but was saved by a visiting Iraqi archaeologist who alerted Yemeni authorities to this treasure. Speaking eloquently of the deep continuities with Arabia's past, it was the most haunting place on our journey.

Overleaf: Old Marib, the capital of the kingdom of Saba. Still lived in today, it is made up of the accumulated debris of three millennia of human habitation.

The last walk. From the ruined temple it is a short stroll up to the top of the mound, and a final scene of dereliction. The great houses are falling into ruins – some are split right open as if an axe has sliced away their walls to reveal floors and interiors. Most of them have collapsed completely, but those still standing all have stone bases made of fine squared stone. There are fragments of masonry everywhere. One house has part of an ibex-head frieze like the one we saw in Yeha. Above another door there is a finely cut inscription in Sabaean script. These are all that is left of the great buildings described by the Greek historian Diodorus of Sicily:

> Since for ages they have never suffered the ravages of war because of their secluded position, and since there is so much gold and silver in their country, especially in Saba where the royal palace is situated, they have embossed goblets of every kind, made of silver and gold, couches and tripods with silver feet, and every other furnishing of incredible costliness, and halls encircled by large columns, some of them gilded and others with silver figures on their capitals. Their ceilings and doors are decorated with sunken recesses set with close packed precious stones. Thus they have made the structure of their houses in every way marvellous for its opulence, for some parts they have made in silver and gold, others of ivory, and the most showy precious stones, or whatever else men esteem most highly.

The mound is entirely artificial, composed of layers of human habitation that have accumulated over the centuries. The destructions and rebuildings, the continual depositing of rubbish and debris, the re-laying of the floors in every generation, have built a mound up to 30 metres deep. So what we see on top of it today is just the end of the process, the product of the last two or three hundred years of life here. Now the water has gone and the houses have decayed. There are about fifteen families still living here, getting water in by car or donkey. A woman dressed in a blue cotton Yemeni veil, floral skirt and black top joins us. Her name is Maryam, and she takes us into her house and up a winding stairway to view the whole site. She tells us that the government evicted most of the people from the site a while ago; those who are left are the poorest of the poor and have nowhere to go. So after more than three thousand years, the life of this place is almost over. When the last people have gone, the archaeologists will slice into the mound and, it is hoped, finally solve the mysteries of Saba.

Maryam's little son sits on the parapet overlooking the dying city. 'That is the palace of King Solomon,' he says, pointing down to the ruined mosque with its giant monoliths from a much earlier age. Somewhere there, perhaps, is the real-life palace of a historical Queen of Saba. The dig will be the great prize of Arabian archaeology and is already being fought over by foreign archaeologists who want to get their hands on it. But I for one will experience a tinge of regret when the last people, like Maryam and her little boy, have left and they demolish the last houses, the ancient mud skyscrapers, that mark old Marib's skyline. For then, after its long history, it will become a dead site and, although the gain in knowledge will no doubt be exciting, the people, who are after all the real connection with the past, will be gone.

EPILOGUE: MYTH AND HISTORY

And that – until the excavations take place – is as far as our search can go. Our journey was over. The next day we set out across the mountains on the road to Sanaa, the great medieval capital of Yemen. After years of isolation, tourism is being encouraged in this beautiful and fascinating land. In the crowded bazaars are heaps of incense and myrrh; and in the tourist shops you can buy portraits of the Queen of Sheba, painted by today's Yemeni artists, in which her face is a modern one. Whereas the Koran and the medieval Christian and Jewish traditions depict her with hairy legs, today's queen is a one-world supermodel of feline grace: young, beautiful and unlined, still framed by the sun and moon in today's heartland of Islam, still possessed of iconic power in a culture that has eschewed the visual image.

Her story affords fascinating insights into the way that a tale can grow from a small historical kernel. It comes no doubt partly from folk tales of a kind known the world over, partly too from the religious fantasies of those who controlled the written texts, whether Jewish, Christian or Muslim. In the medieval West, St Thomas Aquinas even imagines her tale as a parable of the mystical union of male and female. As for the 'kernel', from the short texts in the Bible it is possible (and perhaps permissible) to imagine her as an Iron Age potentate from a South Arabian civilization, which in the late eighth and early seventh centuries sent caravans to the Fertile Crescent; a contemporary then of the historical Hiram of

---

Overleaf: Sanaa, a medieval caravan city and the capital of Yemen.
Perhaps the mansions and palaces of old Marib in its heyday looked something like this.

Tyre and Sennacherib: a queen who perhaps even led an embassy, as did other Arabian queens of her time, to the lands of the Mediterranean and the Near East.

Whether she really met Solomon – if indeed he really existed – is another matter. The fairy-tale elements are there at the very beginning in the Bible story itself: the riddles, the 'never before seen' gifts and the hints of sexual liaison. Perhaps the magical and exotic name of Sheba was simply brought into the tale to add to Solomon's glory; but perhaps an early king of Israel really did meet such an embassy, and had the event recorded in a brief account of his deeds which found its way into the biblical account of Solomon that was constructed some centuries later. As for the later spread of the tale, there are many unknowns. My guess, for what it is worth, is that the story came to Ethiopia with the Bible some time in the early Christian era. This would have most likely been in the fourth century, when Greek-speaking missionaries from Syria came up the route from the Red Sea, and the King of the 'Ethiopians' in Axum became a Christian. I imagine that's when a connection was first made, though in the first century in Palestine the historian Josephus had already said that the queen was 'Ethiopian'. For Ethiopians, the

Above: The incense bazaar in Sanaa. Frankincense and myrrh are still sold here, but the international commerce that drove the incense trail since the opening up of the Near Eastern world in the eighth century BC is now largely gone.

Bible story of the mythic queen whom they could claim as their own could be neatly incorporated into their history. Eventually the hold of the Orthodox Church became so strong that this first link with the Bible shaped itself into a founding myth of the nation, establishing the tale of the bloodline of Solomon and Sheba that is still part of Ethiopia's national story today.

Her appearance in the Muslim tradition as the 'Queen of the South', in the Koran in the seventh century, incorporates the strange story of her hairy leg, which is also found in the Christian tradition of Ethiopia. From then on it is impossible to untangle all the influences. These days Ethiopians are still the most vociferous in claiming her, but with the rediscovery of the lost civilization of Arabia, Yemenis also hold her to be theirs. And both, perhaps, are justified. For her tale has gone far beyond mere historical truth: the legend has become the fact.

At the core of the legend, as the Ethiopian pilgrim told me at the beginning of my journey in Jerusalem, is the tale of the woman of power. African or Arabian, she is the alien and exotic Other. In her stories she has many names but no name: she is a dark-skinned cipher on which almost anything can be read. She is the worshipper of sun, moon and stars, who is co-opted into the patriarchal universe of the 'new' monotheistic faiths; a conversion which not only rescues her for the one true God, but also makes her both fantasy lover and mother. The politics of the tale, then, are cultural, religious and sexual: both in Solomon's temple, and in his bed, she is redeemed from her own former self. Though she gives birth to a son, she takes no husband. She is the eternal female, but her representations in art and fiction reveal ancient stereotypes of race and gender. She is personified Wisdom itself, but her sisters are also the female demons and goddesses whose ancestry goes back to the Babylonian Lilith, queen of the night. Robed in her cloak of stars, she is 'chaste, wise and rich', but with her cloven foot and hairy leg she is dark goddess, demon and femme fatale. But, after all, hasn't that been the fate of so many women of power throughout history – even in our own time?

ARTHUR:
THE ONCE AND
FUTURE KING

PRELUDE: THE STORY-TELLER, OXFORD, 1129

Oxford, where the real and the unreal jostle in the streets, where North Parade is in the south and South Parade is in the north, where Paradise is lost under a pumping station; where the river mists have a solvent and vivifying effect on the stone of the ancient buildings so that the gargoyles of Magdalen College climb down at night and fight with those from Wykeham, or fish under the bridges ... Oxford, where windows open into other worlds ...

OSCAR BAEDECKER *The Coasts of Bohemia* in Philip Pullman *Lyra's Oxford* 2003

THE RAIN FALLS IN A LIGHT DRIZZLE, spattering the oily surface of the canal, and smoke rises in the chill air from the chimneys of barges moored by the towpath.

Over the basin are the crumbling red walls of an old brick factory, the back-to-back houses of Jericho, and the Victorian campanile of St Barnabas Church. This is a place whose fictions are as suggestive as its histories. *Alice in Wonderland*, the *Chronicles of Narnia* and *The Lord of the Rings* were written close by; Jude the Obscure and Inspector Morse walked this path, and Philip Pullman sets his *Northern Lights* in the *Dark Materials* trilogy right here on the bank, among 'the narrow boats and the butty boats … the brick burners' children and the gyptian families who lived in canal-boats, came and went with the spring and autumn fairs'. Out west the Thames has burst its banks in the winter floods, and Port Meadow is a great sheet of water as far as Godstow Nunnery and the fields of Wolvercote, turning the urban industrial landscape back into a medieval wilderness.

Oxford's origins are now obscured by the spread of its suburbs – the Cowley carworks, the university extensions, the well-heeled commuter land of Summertown. In medieval times the town lay sandwiched between the rivers Cherwell and Thames, on a low promontory surrounded by a filigree of streams, lodes and watercourses with obstinately English-sounding names – Bulstake Stream, Hogacre Ditch and Hinkley Stream – beyond which rise the mysterious glades of Wytham Great Wood and Cuddesdon, burial place of a shadowy Saxon chief killed in a sixth-century battle with the Britons.

Leave the muddy towpath and its solvent mists, cross the rain-streaked station car park, walk under the railway line and out over Osney Bridge. Double-decker buses, their lights blazing, bearing schoolchildren and evening shoppers, whoosh by through pools of rainwater. Here, in a Victorian suburb by Bulstake Stream, an industrial estate occupies what was once Osney Island. Tucked away among the houses are the scanty remains of a once grand medieval church beside a derelict mill house, thick with pigeon droppings. Unlikely as it may seem, you have reached the key place in the creation of one of the world's great myths.

It is rare that we can pinpoint the exact time and place of a myth's transformation or reinvention. But it was here at Osney in 1129 that a young cleric of Welsh, or perhaps Breton, descent arrived who would do just that. Oxford monastic documents show that this learned and self-consciously British young man called himself proudly Gaufridus Monemutensis or, more curiously, Geoffrey

Arthur. We know him as Geoffrey of Monmouth, and of all the writers, poets and artists who have contributed to the myths of King Arthur, Geoffrey is the most brilliantly imaginative and influential; as successful as those later Oxford tale-tellers, Carroll, Lewis and Tolkein; for he gave us Guinevere, Merlin and the evil Mordred, Excalibur and Avalon, and the once and future king himself. When Geoffrey put down his pen in Oxford around 1135, what is arguably the greatest single story in the myths of the world was about to take Europe by storm.

THE MYTHS OF THE CELTS

Along with the Greeks and the Indians, the Celts have produced the greatest body of myth in the literature of the world. As we have seen in the other stories in this book, myths are wonderful tales created over time that often contain a kind of distillation of the histories and beliefs of earlier societies: they put us in touch with our deep past psychologically, no matter what overlays have come later through, say, religion or modernity. Myths open up worlds of enchantment, but unlike fairy-tales, which are essentially optimistic, great myths by and large are pessimistic.

The core myths of the Celts centre on the great cycle of stories around King Arthur, the knights of the Round Table, the quest for the Holy Grail, and the break-up of Arthur's order, leading to the final, fateful battle of Camlann, in which the king is mortally wounded. The famous medieval Arthurian romances are full of courage, idealism and passion, but they are shot through with a dark strain of sexual jealousy and betrayal. These tales of Arthur are also connected to an earlier cycle of stories and poems that the Celts called the Matter of Britain, which concerns the fall of Celtic Britain to the Saxons, the ancestors of today's English. These stories link the legend of King Arthur to a common poetic idea of Britain, or Albion, as a kind of paradise land of the West, an ideal landscape with a primeval unspoiled past. Together they add up to the greatest theme in the literature of the British Isles: as we shall see, a British myth, later appropriated by the English, which became a powerful symbol for all living in these islands – and for many more, further afield.

Today the tale has lost none of its appeal in literature and film, and in popular culture. In 2004 another Hollywood Arthurian epic appeared, this time with a grittily realistic Guinevere, daubed in woad, fighting with Sarmatian warriors in a

Opposite: Poster for the 1967 film *Camelot*. The Arthur tale has had a long and strange afterlife: influenced by the original stage production, President Kennedy's court in Washington became known as Camelot.

CAMELOT

mud-streaked Roman twilight. On the screen at the beginning of the film a caption tells us that modern historians have now shown that the story is *true*. As we shall see, that begs a big question. But why is Arthur important to us still, and why was he so important in the past? And where does the myth come from? Do its roots lie in some kernel of history, like other tales in this book; or did it arise out of a much older tradition of tale-telling? Or is it on the other hand the creation of much more recent times, including our own? Those were the questions I carried with me on a journey round the Celtic lands from Cornwall to Wales and southern Ireland, the Western Isles and Brittany, in search of the many incarnations, and the strange transformations, of the once and future king.

THE ROMAN TWILIGHT: 'IN THOSE DAYS ARTHUR FOUGHT WITH THEM'

Great myths – the *Epic of Gilgamesh*, Jason, Troy and the *Mahabharata* among them – are often rooted loosely in real places and real history, and the original Arthurian myth is no different. In the earliest sources the tale is set in real events, perhaps the most momentous events in the history of the British Isles, namely the arrival of Anglo-Saxon-speaking invaders in the fifth century: what came to be called the Coming of the English. There is still much controversy about this, and there are scholars who don't even believe there was an Anglo-Saxon conquest, but think that the archaeological evidence indicates not an invasion but slow assimilation. But this is to ignore literary and poetic evidence of the most compelling kind, including oral traditions which, though only written down later as in other pre-literate societies, were often very tenacious in preserving key events, names of kings and battles, and royal genealogies, even if the precise chronology and dates were forgotten. In any case, to ignore the literary evidence gives us no hope of a narrative: historians, like bards, depend on stories!

Combining the literary and archaeological evidence the story goes like this. On the outer fringe of the Roman empire, Britain from the AD 300s faced the continual threat of invasions and raiding by barbarian war-bands and tribes, including Angles and Saxons from Denmark and Saxony. Massive forts were built around the south and east coast – the 'Saxon Shore' – to repel them. But archaeological evidence shows that Germanic mercenaries were also hired as defence forces, which were often settled around Roman towns. In 410 the overstretched Romans under Honorius refused further aid to the province, and the Romano-Britons were forced to go it alone. Over the next two or three decades the situation perhaps began to

resemble a modern decolonization, with factions, powerful local clans and 'patriotic freedom fronts' fighting among each other and against the encroaching power of the Germanic newcomers. Hadrian's Wall ceased to be garrisoned, although some of its forts became the seats of regional warlords. The cities began to be abandoned, and in the south civic authorities retreated to the old Iron Age hill-forts which were refortified as military bases and refuges for the population.

Around the 440s the pressure from raids had become intense and a letter was sent by a group of British civic authorities to the Roman consul Aetius in Gaul, appealing for military aid. But their request was ignored. Then, says the Byzantine historian Zosimus, the Britons 'fighting for themselves freed their cities from the attacking barbarians' and after repudiating external authority 'were living on their own no longer obedient to Roman laws'. Another mid-century Byzantine writer, Procopius, says, 'the Romans never recovered Britain, which continued to be ruled by tyrants', the usual term for self-styled emperors. The most famous of these was

Above: The Roman fort at Richborough in Kent – the site of the Roman landing in AD 43, the legendary coming of the Saxons in 449, and the arrival of St Augustine in 597.

the 'proud tyrant', identified in Welsh legend as Gwyrtheyrn gwledig, or Vortigern. According to later legend it was Vortigern who took the fateful step of settling Saxon mercenaries on the Isle of Thanet in Kent in order to repel sea-borne marauders. This they did, but more came after them in the hope of richer pickings, and in the end the mercenaries rebelled. Warfare spread across the island as far as the Irish Sea; urban life broke down, and great tracts of the land were devastated from east to west.

This is the context of the myth of the Coming of the English, and it is the background to the first appearance of Arthur. Of the key characters, Vortigern himself seems to have been a real person. The Saxon leaders Hengist and Horsa, 'Mare' and 'Stallion', on the other hand, sound like a tale told by bards, not by historians. However, the later English tradition may be right about their having landed at Ebbsfleet on the edge of the Isle of Thanet, where a now derelict power station stands over reedy backwaters near Sandwich; this is also where early Welsh tradition located the landing. The Anglo-Saxons later dated the Coming of the English to 449: a symbolic date, no doubt, but a moment never to be forgotten in the Celtic world.

Above: The Isle of Thanet, top left, now joined to the coast of Kent. In the myth, the landing of the Saxons was at Ebbsfleet, now on the stream, bottom right.

The events that followed have been part of the mythologies of the English and Celts ever since. For as so often in history, legends were born in a period of dramatic conflict and irrevocable change. In a war of resistance the Saxons were defeated; and in the later legend the British leader was Arthur.

NENNIUS: THE TWELVE BATTLES OF ARTHUR

A Dark Age guerrilla leader, a cavalry commander repelling the Saxon hordes – this is the modern version of Arthur, presented in recent books and films. This first incarnation of Arthur, however, is only recorded well over three hundred years after these events. He first appears in the *History of the Britons*, written in 830, as a heroic British general and a Christian warrior. Attributed to a writer called Nennius, the *History of the Britons* was a riposte to the patronizing English attitude towards Welsh history, and it mixed history and myth with abandon. But the author, who wrote in Latin, probably knew both English and Welsh, and he was able to draw on earlier sources, chronicles and genealogies from both cultures. The scene is the late fifth century: Vortigern is dead, and Anglo-Saxon tribes are attacking Britain. What follows is one of the most pregnant passages in British history:

> Then in those days Arthur fought against them with the kings of the Britons, but he was commander (*dux bellorum*) in those battles.

Nennius then gives a list of twelve battles fought by Arthur: a battle at the mouth of the river Glein; four battles on a river Dubglas 'in the region of Linnuis'; a sixth battle on a river called Bassas; a seventh in the 'Caledonian forest'; further battles were at Guinnion fort, at the 'City of the Legion', on the river Tribruit, and at a hill called Agned; and the twelfth at a place called Badon Hill. The location of these battles is still hotly argued, and they have been placed all over Britain.

For two of the battles Nennius adds further fascinating details which show that by the ninth century the tale was already influenced by legend and bardic story. At the eighth battle, at Guinnion fort, 'Arthur carried the image of the holy Mary, the everlasting virgin, on his shield, and the heathen were put to flight on that day and there was a great slaughter made on them through the power of Our Lord Jesus Christ and the power of the holy Virgin Mary his mother ...' At the twelfth battle, on Badon Hill, 'nine hundred and sixty men fell in one day, from a single charge of Arthur's, and no one laid them low save he alone, and he was victorious in all his campaigns.'

These stories are obviously mythic in character, the Dark Age Che Guevara verging towards the later medieval Superman. A slightly different version of Nennius survives in a Vatican manuscript, written in England in 945, which adds a small but pointed detail: 'Then the warrior Arthur, with the soldiers and the kings of Britain, used to fight against them [i.e. the Saxons]. And *though there were many of more noble birth than he,* he was twelve times leader in war and victor of the battles ...'

Nennius's twelve battles evidently belong to an old tradition of battle-list poems in Welsh poetry. One on the hero Cadwallon, for example, begins: 'He waged fourteen big battles for fair Britain, and sixty skirmishes ...', before listing each one with a brief tag ('on Mount Digoll, seven months and seven battles each day ... he fed eagles ... a lion, terrible in his onslaught ...'). The list of Arthur's battles is similar: some of the battle names appear in early poetry and annals, stretched over a wide period of time and place. The Caledonian forest is clearly northern. The tragic battle at the 'City of the Legion', Chester, in 616 was long remembered in Welsh lore. Badon, as we shall see, was a battle in southern Britain in the 490s. This kind of eclectic plundering of famous battles was the bard's stock-in-trade. The Old English poem of the minstrel Widsith lists tribes and characters from the fourth century to the sixth, piled on each other for effect: 'I was with the Huns and with the glorious Goths, with the Swedes and the Geats, the Angles and the Saxons, rewarded for my song.' One Welsh bard even claims to have seen the battles of Alexander! Wordsmith and spirit raiser, the poet's job is to rise above the constraints of place and time.

So the twelve battles of Arthur are not history. Impossible as one man's war, they are in fact the first signs of a legend. At the end of his text Nennius goes on to talk about the natural marvels of Britain, and identifies some places associated with Arthur in folklore, which suggests that by the ninth century Arthur was already a folk hero.

Another source for the Dark Age Arthur is the *Annals of Wales*. In origin these are older than Nennius: a series of brief annals probably originally entered in Latin by monks into their Easter tables. These incorporate some genuine notes from the fifth and sixth centuries, but the surviving text is in a manuscript dating from the twelfth century which is copied from one made in South Wales in 955. In it there are two references to Arthur. Again there is the battle of Badon, but there

---

Opposite: There is no one Age of Arthur, so it is hard to draw a map to represent the myth. This shows the key places on our journey, and the main sites associated with the Arthur myth.

is also the first tantalizing appearance of the famous battle in which Arthur is killed – a crucial part of the tale from Geoffrey of Monmouth to Malory, Tennyson and Hollywood.

> 516
> The battle of Badon in which Arthur carried the cross of our Lord Jesus Christ for three days and nights on his shoulders [*in humeros suos* but probably mistranslating the Welsh for 'on his shield'] and the Britons were the victors.

> 537
> The battle at Camlann in which Arthur and Medraut fell; and there was plague in Britain and Ireland.

So here in one teasingly allusive line is Medraut, the original Mordred, Arthur's nephew who finally betrays him; and the final disaster in which Arthur is fatally wounded: what Tennyson calls the 'last, dim, weird battle of the west'.

The dates are not reliable, but the next entry, '547 A great mortality', probably refers to the great plague that swept the Roman empire in the 540s. So where do these entries come from? These annals were written in Latin; however, the story about Arthur bearing the cross on his back, which is paralleled in Nennius, sounds as if it was taken from a poetic source in Welsh. The original set of annals was probably laconic in the extreme and maybe simply noted the Badon and Camlann battles, though interestingly the 537 entry uses the Welsh word for battle (*gueith*), suggesting that perhaps it also came from a poetic source.

The third and last source on the early Arthur is the *Gododdin*, a marvellous poem composed in the Scottish borders in the late sixth century by the bard Aneirin. It concerns an ill-fated and ultimately tragic attack on the Saxons at Catraeth (Catterick) in which three hundred British heroes died. Among the heroes one is praised for his bravery 'though he was no Arthur'. If we could prove this line was written in the sixth century, then obviously that might be a pointer to the date – and the place? – of the early Arthur legend, but unfortunately this phrase is not in the earliest copies of the poem and may have been added at a later date, perhaps in the ninth century.

Suggestive and alluring as these texts are, to a historian none of them is anywhere near to being a primary source. So how did the idea of a historical Arthur fighting the Saxons in around AD 500 come about? The key is the connection made

in Nennius and the *Annals of Wales* between Arthur and the battle of Badon. For the siege of Mons Badonicus, or Badon Hill, was unquestionably a real event, the heroic final stand of the 'last of the Romans'.

ARTHUR AND THE BATTLE OF BADON

From the windy summit of Liddington Castle the paragliders circle slowly in the air currents like huge red and blue butterflies. From the lip of the earth ramparts, to the north there are wonderful views towards the Cotswolds and the middle Thames valley. Liddington is an Iron Age hill-fort on the northern edge of a prominent upland that stands out between the Berkshire and Marlborough downs, in an area where other battles of the sixth century took place. Right below the hill is the prehistoric Great Ridgeway heading from the Chilterns down to Avebury; to the west lorry traffic roars down Ermine Street from Cirencester to Winchester; to the east is the Roman road to Silchester. The site has been one of the strategic road junctions of southern Britain for millennia, and it was the front line in the wars of

Above: The view from Liddington Castle towards the Thames valley – and possible site of Badon Hill. At the bottom of the hill, running along the line of trees, is the prehistoric Great Ridgeway.

the late fifth and early sixth centuries, situated between the heartland of the Britons and the Saxon chiefdoms of the Thames valley.

Frustratingly, no one has yet been able to locate Badon with certainty. Nennius identifies it with Bath, but surely mistakenly (Badon is a Celtic name, Bath is the Anglo-Saxon name for the Roman town of Aquae Sulis). However, the fact that the battle was a siege of a hill strongly suggests that, like other battles of the time, it took place at a hill-fort. We don't know the name of Liddington Castle in the late Roman period, but in Anglo-Saxon times it bore the name Baddeburi, which could derive from the *burh*, or fort, of Badon. Nearby too is Baydon, an ancient village surrounded by Celtic and Romano-British fields. If anywhere, one would think, the battle was fought here. It was a great victory for the Britons, which is why it was remembered by later bards and chroniclers, who claimed that Arthur had been the leader. And, as it happens, there is a near-contemporary source for the battle, one of the most important narratives in British history. The book was written by a Welsh cleric called Gildas and it is called *On the Ruin of Britain*.

'THIS SCEPTRED ISLE': GILDAS AND THE IDEA OF BRITAIN

To later chroniclers such as Bede and William of Malmesbury, Gildas was simply the 'historian of the Britons'. He was a British priest who probably wrote in the 540s, though possibly a decade or so earlier. Gildas was not writing a history, but a political and religious diatribe, a scathing attack on the rulers of his time. He talks of Britain as his *patria* (fatherland) and the British as *cives* (fellow citizens) – a word related to a term still in use in modern Welsh today, *cymry*. Gildas represents the first British literary response to the English, and in his pages some of the great themes of British history are outlined in an almost Shakespearean plea for unity and order.

As the title of his book shows, Britain is Gildas's real theme. No mere historian, Gildas has a prophetic vision in keeping with many later Welsh poems. At the centre stands the island of Britain personified as a woman. After God she is the most important figure in his story, conveying to his readers and to posterity a conception of the unity of Britain that becomes central to later Welsh poetry and polemic, and, through Geoffrey of Monmouth, to the great medieval Arthurian literature: a Britain of the poets, which has shaped our imaginations – and our emotions – from that day to this.

This idea of a female Britannia ravaged by the forces of evil and disorder because of the moral failings of the people will be one of the great ideas behind the

Arthurian tales, even when they are no longer seen as battles between Britons and Saxons, but as conflicts of good versus evil. The key passage in Gildas is set in the period between the 450s and the 490s. The land has been devastated by the Saxons from sea to sea. Then, at this desperate pass, cometh the hour, cometh the man.

GILDAS, AMBROSIUS AND ARTHUR

> After some time passed, when the cruel plunderers [the Saxons] had gone back to their homes, God gave strength to the survivors [the Britons fighting the invaders]. Wretched people fled to them from all directions … and begged that they should not be altogether destroyed. Their leader was Ambrosius Aurelianus, a gentleman who, almost alone of the Romans, had survived the shock of this huge catastrophe (certainly his parents, who had worn the purple, were killed in it). His descendants in our day have become greatly inferior to their grandfather's excellence. Under him our people regained their strength and challenged the victors to battle; and with God's will they won the victory. From that time now our countrymen won, then the enemies, so that in this people the Lord could make trial (as he does) of this latter-day Israel to see whether it loves him or not. This lasted right up to the year of the siege of Badon Hill, pretty well the last defeat of the hated ones, and certainly not the least. That was the year of my birth; as I know, one month of the forty-fourth year since then has already passed.

There are few more tantalizing passages in British history. Though the British commander at the battle of Badon is not specifically named by Gildas, their chief leader in the war against the Saxons is not Arthur but Ambrosius. Gildas tells us that this man was of an important Roman noble family, people who had 'worn the purple' – so perhaps Ambrosius belonged to the Ambrosii (as did St Ambrose of Milan whose father was called Aurelianus Ambrosius), who had been rulers in Gaul in the fourth century. The Romano-British Ambrosius and his family are not known from any other early source, but some memory of their exploits came down to Nennius, who mentions their conflict with the tyrant Vortigern. Ambrosius (Welsh Emrys) also lies behind the strange legend told by Nennius and Geoffrey of Monmouth about the boy with prophetic powers, the 'child with no father' who was brought to be sacrificed by the tyrant Vortigern. The boy appears in other Welsh traditions as Embreis Guletic, Emrys (or Ambrosius) 'the overlord', and

Nennius tells us that his father was 'one of the consuls of the Roman people'. But Geoffrey splits him in two, to make Merlin-Emrys, whose prophecies foretell the coming of Arthur.

According to Gildas, though, writing only forty-four years after the battle of Badon, it is Ambrosius who is the key historical figure in the wars of the mid to late fifth century. And it is therefore significant that in early Welsh tradition it is

Above: Ambrosius reading his prophecies to the tyrant Vortigern. Both these legendary characters are based on real figures in the fifth-century history of Britain.

Ambrosius and Vortigern who are at the centre of the myths surrounding these events; Arthur only comes later. The real Ambrosius is still a mystery, and there may be more to discover about him. His name appears to have survived in the Wiltshire town of Amesbury, in Old English Ambresburh, 'the fortress of Ambrosius' (referring to the big Iron Age fort known locally as Vespasian's Camp). An important Anglo-Saxon royal estate, Amesbury parish also contains the most remarkable collection of Bronze Age antiquities in Britain, among them Stonehenge: the greatest of all monuments to the power of the prehistoric rulers of southern Britain. One wonders whether it is a coincidence that the fort associated with the leader of the British wars in the fifth century should be adjacent to Stonehenge?

But if Ambrosius was the leader in the war, where does that leave Arthur? If Arthur won twelve battles which climaxed at Badon Hill; if he bore the cross on his back, and killed hordes of pagan Saxons, then it is strange that he is not mentioned in Gildas's account of the battle. Arguments from silence are never entirely satisfactory, of course, but on the face of it, no source before the ninth century mentions Arthur as a war leader against the Saxons, and none in a form or context that can safely be taken as historical. The twelve battles of Arthur look like later poetic conflation. Our one contemporary source from the sixth century, Gildas, does not mention him and tells us that the British leader in these battles was called Ambrosius. The case for a fifth- or sixth-century Arthur fighting Anglo-Saxons in southern Britain looks decidedly flimsy. He is simply not there. So who was Arthur? And *where* was Arthur?

ARTHUR: THE BEGINNING OF THE MYTH?

So far in this detective story we have found that the legend of Arthur as a heroic Christian warrior starts in the ninth century in Nennius's pseudo-history. Partly perhaps a product of Nennius's own imagination, Arthur begins as a Celtic folk hero: a response to the growing power of the English – and to the growing realization by the Celts that the invaders were here to stay.

Out of these intriguing hints in old chronicles and poems we can begin to see too how myths can emerge out of a kernel of real events, folk tales, local legends and political prophecy. Whether Arthur was a historical character was of no concern to earlier writers. It is still possible, however, that there was some historical figure who gave his name to the hero, a real Arthur lurking somewhere in the shadowy world of Dark Age Britain (perhaps in the north?), a man whose name at least was passed down by the bards and story-tellers. To that fascinating subject we will return.

'THE BRITONS WILL RISE AGAIN': PROPHECY FROM NENNIUS TO GEOFFREY OF MONMOUTH

So by the ninth century Arthur was a hero, though not a king, who beat the Saxons and for a time held back the flood. The growth of his legend was in response to the cultural and political needs of the time, just as the Arthurs of Geoffrey of Monmouth, Malory, Spenser and Tennyson would be. But his story was part of a bigger theme: the Matter of Britain.

By Nennius's time – the Viking Age – the subjugation of lowland Britain had been achieved by the Anglo-Saxons, and a number of small kingdoms had been established. These kingdoms had adopted Christianity and had developed a sense of identity as an English nation. Taking a leaf out of Gildas's book, their historian Bede had portrayed the English as a chosen people destined to rule the island of Britain, which the Celts had lost because of God's judgement on their failings. The Matter of Britain now had a rival: the Matter of England.

We can tap the mood of that time in a wonderful Welsh poem of the late ninth century which takes us to dark and stormy nights on the coast of Wales at the fortress of Tenby. To while away the long winter evenings in his royal hall, with the spray beating on the shutters, the King of Dyfed would turn to the manuscripts in his 'book room' and to his bards and praise singers. At such times, the poet says, 'The Matter of Britain was the chief object of care'. He is talking about the sixth-century poems of Aneirin, Taliesin and Myrddin, the ancient prophecies and books such as Nennius's *History of the Britons*: ammunition in the wars with the English; exemplars of action, and of consolation.

Just how these political and cultural struggles were reflected in the literature of the day is neatly revealed by two tenth-century poems from either side of the racial divide. Still fondly hoping for the overthrow of the English, a Welsh cleric in South Wales wrote the *Great Prophecy of Britain* – the greatest of all Welsh prophetic poems, which would serve as a literary model for Merlin's prophecy of Arthur in Geoffrey of Monmouth's work. In it Myrddin, the prototype of Merlin, foretells that the Welsh will rise up, and with the help of the Irish, Scots, Bretons and Cornish – the old Celtic world united once more – will drive the English 'pale faces' out 'at Aber Sandwich' (where they had first landed). 'We will pay them back for the 404 years,' he wrote, 'and the Britons will rise again.' When these hopes were crushed at the battle of Brunanburh, an Old English poet gloated in his turn: 'Never was there such a victory since the Angles and Saxons first sailed over the broad waves, sought out Britain, overcame the Welsh, and seized the land.' So both poets harked back to the Coming of the English. However, the Welshman had called not on Arthur but on the heroes Cynan and Cadwalladr as the chieftains who would drive the English out. In the tenth century, then, Arthur was the focus of many local legends but not yet a pan-British hero. But his time was about to come. Soon enough the prophesies would become attached to him.

THE NORMAN CONQUEST: 'ARTHUR IS NOT DEAD'

In 1066 England fell to the Normans, who soon invaded the Celtic kingdoms too, and in the later 1100s began the attack on Ireland, initiating a chain of bloody events whose aftermath only began to be untangled in the twentieth century. It was in the first generations after the Norman Conquest that the Matter of Britain began to be articulated in myth and literature as a central theme in the mainstream culture; we are now entering the great phase of Arthurian myth-making.

Myths and legends are often crystallized in interesting times, times of crisis or opportunity. And the early twelfth century was certainly that. Without doubt 1066 had been a disaster for everyone in the British Isles, but for all the cruelty and devastation the arrival of the Normans unleashed tremendous cultural energies, initiating exchanges and contacts, especially with the French-speaking world, that would transform the Arthurian tales.

The 1130s were a time of anarchy, violence and war in England and the Celtic lands. The Norman subjugation of Wales had gone on apace, despite Welsh protests that they were 'trying to wipe out the British so well that even the name be forgotten'.

The military war was also accompanied by a cultural war on the Celts, who were pictured as barbarians in need of civilizing. As a French writer put it, 'the Welsh are savage by nature, wilder than the beasts in the field.' These political and cultural struggles came to a head in the great Welsh revolt of the 1130s, when the rebels hoped 'to restore the British kingdom'. There were dramatic reverses for the Anglo-Norman occupiers: their leaders were killed, their armies defeated, castles taken and large tracts of Wales reclaimed. The mood of the time in Wales is crystallized in a poetic text of the 1130s: 'The Welsh openly go around saying that in the end they will have it all … through Arthur they will get it back … They will call it Britain again.'

These were grassroots ideas whose origins lay far back in time. Arthur had in fact already been claimed in the previous century by Welsh nationalists, who also believed that he would one day return. 'Marvellous stories of King Arthur have been noised about this mighty realm so far and wide,' said one French writer, 'that the truth has turned to fable and idle songs.' A group of well-heeled and supercilious French clerics on a tour of Cornwall were shouted down and physically threatened in Bodmin when they laughed at the locals' claims that 'the king is not dead but will return: that Britain will rise again'.

THE NEW HISTORY: 'ALL THE BRITONS HAVE ARE FABLES ON ARTHUR'

So Arthur was now part of the British rhetoric of resistance. Not surprisingly this excited the curiosity of the writers of the day, in particular the new generation of historians who were writing to help the new foreign rulers understand the history of the lands they had appropriated. And the issue of Arthur and the Celtic past now excited these 'new historians': second-generation Normans – men like Henry of Huntingdon and especially William of Malmesbury. Despite the fact that he had an English mother, William was a toffee-nosed and ardent Francophile and his was the hot history book of the early 1130s. His history of Britain was entitled *The Deeds of the English Kings*, and in it he made it quite clear what he thought about the 'tainted race of the Britons' and their history. 'All that the Britons could muster were fables on Arthur,' said William loftily. 'There was need for a true history about them. As for the Britons in general, they would have sunk without trace in the memory of other nations had it not been for Gildas …' (Gildas even then had been dead for the best part of six hundred years!) The new historiography of Britain, then, was to be English, just as its future was English. Forget the 'fable and idle songs' about Arthur. The new heroes – and they were real ones – were the kings of England. The British world was England's now.

GEOFFREY OF MONMOUTH

For young Geoffrey of Monmouth, sitting in his library on Osney Island in Oxford, such ideas were like a red rag to a bull. Geoffrey apparently came from Monmouthshire, perhaps from near Caerleon on Usk, 30 kilometres from Monmouth, a Roman town which is mentioned over a dozen times in his book and which he identifies as Arthur's Camelot. His literary career, however, took place not in Wales but in Oxford, where he lived all his working life, from 1129 to 1151.

It was there that he constructed one of the literary smash hits of the Middle Ages: the *History of the Kings of Britain*. Writing from what he calls the 'heart

of Britain' – he never once mentions 'England' – he set out to provide the British with a new national mythology masquerading as history. But where English historians such as Bede and William of Malmesbury had attempted to do the same thing within the confines of historical data – albeit directed and given meaning by Christian ideology and God's miraculous interventions in human affairs – Geoffrey cut loose from mere historical fact. He claimed to have discovered a lost

Above: The coronation of Arthur by Matthew Paris (c. 1250). Early versions of the legend say Arthur was not a king but a 'leader of battles'.

history of the Celts which he alone had read and translated, and which was the authority behind his saga of two thousand years and ninety-nine kings – a panorama as fabulous as the near-contemporary Ethiopian Book of Kings that we met with the Queen of Sheba. Starting in 1115 BC (note the confident precision!), this was Celtic history as people dreamed it might have been – and as it still perhaps could be.

On the way Geoffrey gives us a gallery of characters, many of whom became stars in their own right in the literature of the Middle Ages and Renaissance: Cymbeline, Bladud, Leir and Merlin among them. Right at the centre was the figure of Arthur, now king. In Geoffrey's pages Arthur is a hero who bestrides Europe like a colossus: a Napoleon of the Roman twilight. For the first time his whole life is told: his birth at Tintagel, the son of Uther Pendragon; his battles, and his campaigns in Europe; his eventual betrayal. There's Guinevere and Merlin, and the treacherous Mordred; there's Caliburn, the future Excalibur; and even the king's final resting place at Avalon.

To add verisimilitude and local colour, Geoffrey also cleverly used local legends and folk tales about sites with Arthurian associations. For example, travelling in the southwest he seems to have heard a story about Tintagel as the birthplace of Arthur, and his tale of Arthur's conception by Uther Pendragon is enriched with circumstantial local detail: he mentions, for example, the fortified camp at Dimilioc, 8 kilometres from Tintagel, today's Castle Dameliock. The Cornish tourist industry, for one thing, would never look back.

Even in his own day Geoffrey was attacked by English historians as a 'spinner of tall stories which should be rubbished by everyone'. As for the lost manuscript, which he claimed as the basis for his book – the secret history of the kings of the Britons which he alone had been able to examine – this surely is as tongue-in-cheek as the manuscript in Moorish script that supposedly gave Cervantes his tale of Don Quixote. Lost manuscripts have an honourable tradition in fictional literature, right down to Borges and Umberto Eco; and as a device to torpedo the smug Anglo-centricity of the likes of William of Malmesbury, Geoffrey's worked a treat. The Celts might have lost the political war in the Middle Ages, but they would win the literary battle hands down.

ARTHUR OF THE BRITONS

So, fantasy it may be, but Geoffrey of Monmouth's book is the real creator of Arthur as we know him. Moreover, one of Geoffrey's themes, which recycled the political rhetoric of his own day, would be crucial for the future. At the centre of

his tale is an extended sequence of Merlin's prophecies culminating in the omen of 'a star appearing in the sky, its head like a dragon from whose mouth two beams came at an angle, one across Gaul, one towards Ireland: and the beam of light was Arthur himself and the kingship of Britain'. After the fateful last battle, and the wounded Arthur's journey to Avalon, in a literary master-stroke Geoffrey leaves us

Above: Tintagel Castle, the birthplace of Arthur in Geoffrey of Monmouth's version of the story, and popularly known as such today.

in suspense: perhaps Arthur is not dead. An angelic voice assures the Celts that 'the British people would reoccupy the island in the future, once the appointed moment would come'.

And did he really believe that? Reality, unfortunately always intrudes. After all, Geoffrey was a modern man in Oxford in the mid-1130s; the facts of contemporary history spoke for themselves. So, after all the literary fireworks Geoffrey ends on a curious note of disappointment and defeat for the Britons (coloured perhaps by the crushing of the Welsh revolt in 1138 as he wrote?). The Saxons had won and now were 'opposed only by those pitiful remnants of Britons who dwelt in the forests of Wales … Britons who now called themselves not Britons but Welsh'. He ends with a reflection worthy of Gildas: 'And the Welsh, once they had degenerated from the noble state enjoyed by the Britons, never afterwards recovered the overlordship of the island.'

Geoffrey plainly could not escape the curve of history as seen in the late 1130s. These days his brilliant fantasia on early British history is often seen as an academic leg-pull, a playful *jeu d'esprit*. But Geoffrey launched Arthur and the Matter of Britain into a stratosphere of myth which it has occupied ever since.

AFTER GEOFFREY

So Arthur of Britain was born. In its own day Geoffrey's book had a tremendous influence: over two hundred manuscripts survive today – more than there are of Bede's work – and it had as big an impact in Europe as in Britain. Geoffrey seized the imagination of Europe, inspiring medieval romancers and chroniclers from Chrétien de Troyes and the courtly love poets to the German Wolfram von Eschenbach, and on down to Malory, Spenser, Shakespeare, Dryden, Tennyson, William Morris and the Pre-Raphaelites.

Like Tolkein and C.S. Lewis (both of them, by the way, scholars of medieval and Arthurian literature), Geoffrey had hit on a popular form of serious entertainment which, as one modern commentator has remarked, 'in our post-modernist world is the best any of us historians can hope to provide'. And, of course, it is true that if it were submitted as a script for a cinema film or a TV drama serial now, Geoffrey's book would be a lot easier to sell than Bede's providential tale, so conspicuously lacking in irony. It is dazzling 'infotainment' – much more exciting than mere historical fact – and not surprisingly it reached a bigger audience than other books of the time, just as books on the Holy Grail, the Lost Ark and Da Vinci's code do better today than more sober histories.

THE ISLE OF AVALON: ARTHUR DISCOVERED

There are few more atmospheric places in Britain than Glastonbury. The dramatic green pyramid of the Tor rises over the ancient wetlands of the Somerset levels, crowned with the lonely tower of the medieval church of St Michael. The ruined remains of the ancient abbey date back to the seventh century, some say earlier, and are built over the site of a Roman mausoleum. It's a place where myths and legends abound: the story that it is the oldest Christian site in Britain was first recorded in the tenth century; and later story-tellers embellished the tale with Joseph of Arimathea, St Patrick and the Holy Grail. Even Jesus himself. And the next stage of the growth of the Arthur legend also brings us to Glastonbury or, as the tourist board road signs say as you enter the town, 'The ancient isle of Avalon'.

Above: The atmospheric wetlands of the Somerset levels with Glastonbury Tor beyond. Identified with the legendary Isle of Avalon in the twelfth century, this was where the bones of Arthur and Guinevere were 'discovered' in 1191.

We have begun to see how the Arthur tales grew, out of a 'historical kernel' of real events maybe, but also fuelled by fantasy, folk traditions and the sheer literary chutzpah of the likes of Geoffrey of Monmouth. By the thirteenth century Arthur had become a pan-British hero. Sites associated with him were pointed out from Scotland to Cornwall, and the poems known as the Welsh Triads asserted that he had held his courts in Cornwall, Wales *and* Scotland. Geoffrey's tale had turned him into a historical person, and it was only a matter of time before someone tried to find him – especially in a climate where political radicals and terrorists claimed that he would rise again and drive the English out. This was what led to the search for his grave.

Various burial places of Arthur existed in folk tales and local legends up and down the country. Geoffrey had named Avalon as the place where the wounded Arthur was taken after the fateful last battle of Camlann. In Welsh and Irish myth, Avalon, the Isle of Apples, is an earthly paradise, the land on 'the other side'. Geoffrey did not identify it with any specific place – but it was only a small step to do so. Within a few years of Geoffrey's book the idea arose that Avalon was Glastonbury, and it was there in 1191, in perhaps Britain's earliest recorded archaeological dig, that Arthur's tomb was 'discovered'.

Almost as in a police investigation, the monks conducted their dig behind screens to keep out prying eyes, between two old Saxon stone crosses in the abbey cemetery. The chronicler Gerald of Wales says that the place had been revealed 'by strange and miraculous signs'. Monks had had nocturnal visions, and there were even stories that King Henry II himself had ordered the exhumation, having apparently acquired secret information from 'an ancient Welsh bard, a singer of the past', who said that they would find the body at least 16 feet (5 metres) beneath the earth, not in a tomb of stone but in a hollowed oak: 'And the reason why the body was placed so deep and hidden away is this: that it might never be discovered by the Saxons, who occupied the island after his death, whom he had so often in his life defeated and almost utterly destroyed ...'

Sure enough, about 5 metres down, in a hollowed oak, they found the body of a big man and the bones of a woman with him ... and a lead cross, engraved with the inscription: 'Here lies buried the renowned King Arthur, with Guinevere his second wife, in the Isle of Avalon.'

Opposite: The ruins of the great abbey church at Glastonbury, which a tenth-century tradition claimed as the oldest Christian church in Britain.
Overleaf: St Michael's chapel on Glastonbury Tor. The story that the Holy Grail is buried at its foot at the Chalice Well does not appear in any medieval source, and was made famous by Tennyson in the nineteenth century.

With Arthur's rapidly growing status as folk hero, tourist draw and political rallying cry, it was perhaps inevitable that the English establishment should have wanted to find him. That way they could hit at least two birds with one stone: both prove him dead, and reinvent him as a tourist object. The discovery of the grave in 1191 also took place, coincidentally or not, after a fire had badly damaged the abbey. The restoration fund needed a boost, and finding the burial place at Glastonbury provided it. As businessmen, medieval abbots were nothing if not pragmatic.

But could the Glastonbury skeleton really have been Arthur? Some modern historians have argued that it was. Sadly, however, the evidence is against them. The lead cross has since disappeared, but it was illustrated by the antiquarian Camden in 1695, and to judge by the letter forms in his engraving it was made in the twelfth century. The references in the inscription to 'King Arthur' and to Geoffrey's 'Isle of Avalon' point the same way. Moreover, modern re-excavation of the area located the hole dug in 1191, and revealed the remains of two or three slab-lined graves at the bottom, dating from the seventh century. The monks, one guesses, had simply dug up one of their predecessors.

Although the 1191 exhumation was a fake, it marks the appropriation of Arthur and Guinevere by the English. With hymns and prayers, Arthur's bones would later be reburied inside the abbey in a costly black marble shrine before the altar, in the presence of Edward I and Queen Eleanor, like the holiest of sacred relics. From this time on he would gradually cease to be a Welsh rallying cry – other heroes, more firmly based in historical reality, such as Llewellyn the Great or Owain Glyndower, would take his place. Meanwhile the exhumation only accelerated the spread of Arthur's cult, which became all-pervasive from the late twelfth century onwards. Indeed, the next phase of Arthur's tale moves to the Continent.

THE FRENCH CONNECTION

A lovely late autumn day over Mont-Saint-Michel: pale, silvery light flits with the clouds across the wide, white sands of the bay; slender pinnacles are reflected in the pools left by the tide. In a daffodil sky the sun glitters on the gilded angel standing on the highest spire. With its giant curtain walls, turrets and buttresses, this is everyone's idea of a fairy-tale castle. But Mont-Saint-Michel is not a fortress,

Opposite: Mont-Saint-Michel and its landscape became the focus for many Breton and French Arthurian legends in the twelfth century.

despite the mossy towers rooted round its base. A monastery founded in the eighth century, it grew in size over the centuries to the present labyrinth of chambers, staircases, chapels, refectories, dormitories and scriptoria: 'a liturgy in stone', the father observes as he leads me down to vespers in a subterranean chapel decorated with crumbling frescoes of the eleventh century. If we were to imagine Camelot, this surely would be it.

Below the precinct of the abbey, a tiny town clusters inside the wall protected by a watergate with portcullis and drawbridge. Modern pilgrims stay, as pilgrims did in the past, in a little street lined with half-timbered medieval *auberges* and merchant houses. Like the whole of the Breton peninsula, the place is soaked in Arthurian legend. A mile or two into the bay, for example, is the small hermit's island of Tombelaine, where Arthur overcame a fearsome giant that had killed the daughter of the Duke of Brittany. In the twelfth century, it was said, you could be cursed and stoned for denying that Arthur would soon return. 'You see,' says our Breton guide, as convinced as any Cornishman, 'this is Arthur country.'

Arthur's French connection began soon after the Norman Conquest. In the twelfth century a renaissance took place in western Europe, driven on the one hand by the political power of the English kingdom (a French-speaking kingdom of course) and on the other by the cultural power of France. This is symbolized in the marriage of Henry II of England and the vivacious and beautiful Eleanor of Aquitaine, the divorced wife of Louis VII of France and mother of Richard the Lionheart. In this heady atmosphere poets and troubadours transformed the Arthur legend from a political fable to a tale of chivalric romance. The most powerful of the new twists given to the tale at this time came from French writers. Most important among these was Chrétien de Troyes, who worked for Eleanor's daughter Marie de Champagne. It would be Chrétien who turned the legend from courtly romance into spiritual quest.

THE GRAIL QUEST: THE TALE OF CHRÉTIEN DE TROYES

Chrétien wrote several tales of Arthur and his knights, but in the last one, written in around 1190 and left unfinished at his death, he introduced a new and wonderful element. The knight Perceval, young and inexperienced, is wandering in an unknown land ravaged by war. Searching for shelter for the night, he enters a magical castle ('from here to Beirut you would not have found a more handsome one,' writes Chrétien). The castle is unprotected and its mysterious lord is wounded. Told to sit back and watch, Perceval then sees a haunting vision:

> A boy came in holding a white lance by the middle of the shaft, and he passed in front of the fire. Everyone in the hall saw the white lance with its white head, as a drop of blood issued from the tip of the lance's head, and the red drop ran right down to the boy's hand. Then two other boys appeared bearing candlesticks of the finest gold inlaid with black enamel. In each one burned ten candles at the very least. Now a girl came in, fair and comely and beautifully adorned, and between her hands she held a grail. And when she carried the grail in, the hall was suffused by a light so brilliant that the candles lost their brightness as do the moon or stars when the sun rises. After her came another girl bearing a silver trencher. The grail was made of the finest pure gold, and in it were set precious stones of many kinds, the richest and most precious in the earth or the sea.

Perceval is desperate to know the meaning of the vision, 'who was served from the grail', but earlier in his adventure he was warned by an old knight not to talk too much, and he holds his tongue. That night a feast is held for him in the hall and again 'the grail passed right before his eyes … and he did not know who was served from it, and he longed to know'.

In the morning Perceval wakes up to find the castle eerily empty, its people gone. Thinking they are in the forest, Perceval goes after them 'to see if any could tell him why the lance bled, if perhaps something was wrong, and where the grail had been taken'. He searches and calls out again and again. 'But he was wasting his time calling out like this, for nobody would answer him.'

Perceval never learns the answer to his questions. Very likely we will never know what Chrétien meant by the strange vision. There are vague suggestions in his tale that the land of the grail is ravaged by war and injustice, and that human suffering will continue so long as humankind fails to act with the highest moral courage. But it is Chrétien's vision of the grail itself that captured the imagination of every writer after him. Even though his grail is pictured as a shallow serving dish, later poets made it the cup used by Jesus at the last supper, sometimes elided with the cup in which Mary Magdalene collected his blood at the crucifixion. For the next three centuries this idea fired thinkers and poets across Europe, giving birth on the way to the Glastonbury legends, and the fabulous tales of the great German

epics – Wolfram von Eschenbach's *Parzifal* and Albrecht von Sharfenberg's *Titurel*. These in turn inspired Wagner's *Parsifal* and such strange by-products as the Nazis' grail castle at Wewelsburg, not to mention one of Hollywood's biggest grossing films of all time, *Indiana Jones and the Last Crusade*.

So with Chrétien the idea of the Holy Grail was born. Chrétien's image of the grail, luminous and other-worldly, became a mystical symbol of all human quests, of the human yearning for something beyond, infinitely desirable and yet ultimately unattainable. And with that the Arthur legend enters the true realm of myth.

Above: *The Achievement of the Grail* (1891–4), a tapestry based on *The Quest for the Holy Grail* by Sir Edward Burne Jones. The idea that the grail was Christ's cup at the Last Supper took the Middle Ages by storm. This Victorian version of the myth shows the grail as a cup, though its earliest representation was as a flat serving dish.

ROUND TABLES AND GREEN KNIGHTS

Chrétien's tales caught the imagination of his age. And with the idea of the quest came the idea of the knighthood – and the Round Table. Other writers now created full-scale literary versions of the myth, sometimes with fabulous embellishments. Of these Robert de Boron was the first to mention the Round Table, which now became the structuring metaphor: binding together the disparate 'histories' of the legend, and symbolizing both high-minded fellowship and tragically flawed chivalric order – as well as the ambiguous majesty of kingship itself. The table is depicted in thirteenth-century art rather like the table of the Last Supper, part of the progressive Christianizing of the story after Chrétien. Such tales proliferated in the thirteenth and fourteenth centuries, clearly responding to a psychological need in the courtly audience, and they spawned Arthurian relics: the Winchester Round Table, for example, the most magnificent Arthurian relic, was originally created for King

Edward I for a knightly tournament in 1290. The popularity of the tales also gave rise to real-life chivalric orders such as the Knights of the Garter and, the most curious Arthurian cross-over, the Burgundian order of Jason and the Golden Fleece!

The settings for these tales were always shaped by local legend. Chrétien, for example, used Breton Arthurian legends of the forest of Brocéliande, and the well of Barenton, as the setting for his *Yvain* – the wonderful tale of Sir Owain and the Lady of the Fountain, which is also found in the Welsh *Mabinogion*. A great English Arthurian poem, *Sir Gawain and the Green Knight*, was written for a late fourteenth-century Cheshire family. In it the Castle of Hautdesert becomes a well-known local landmark, Beeston Castle, on its great crag in the north Cheshire plain; and the bleak and atmospheric ravine at Ludchurch is the lonely valley of the Green Chapel. Here Gawain confronts the Green Knight, the Lord of Death, in a tale about the soul's conquest of evil, one with close parallels in Irish myth.

We all seek and make our own Camelots. Chrétien's symbols contributed not only to a cycle of great popular tales but also to an esoteric Christian mystical myth, perhaps even incorporating pre-Christian ideas into the mainstream of Christian culture. By now the legend had gone so far beyond its beginnings that they were no longer recognizable – except perhaps for the dim and distant shadow of Nennius's Christian warrior?

ARTHUR AND THE TUDORS

> ... for thus the Powers reveal;
> That when the Norman Line in strength shall lastly fail
> (Fate limiting the time) th' ancient Britan race
> Shall come again to sit upon the sovereign place

So Shakespeare's friend Michael Drayton reinterpreted the ancient prophecies of Merlin in Geoffrey of Monmouth. In the sixteenth century these prophecies were said to have been fulfilled by the return of a British dynasty to be rulers of Britain: the Tudors, who claimed descent from the true Welsh line of Brutus and Arthur. The British myth was reborn, and Arthur was again a political story.

The founder of the Tudor line, Henry VII, had read his Arthur in the version by Thomas Malory, the last of the great medieval transformations of the tale. Malory, who died in prison in 1471, had reworked the great French romances back into English and added his own mournful commentary on the death of the Age of Chivalry. Born soon after Agincourt, he had fought in the Hundred Years War in his teens and seen the collapse of English power in Europe. He had also seen the failure of rulership at first hand in the Wars of the Roses. These concerns were mirrored, as always, in the Arthurian tale. Malory's *Death of Arthur* is a haunting vision of a knightly golden age swept away by civil strife and the betrayal of its ideals.

Malory's was one of the first books printed in English by Caxton in 1486. Malory identified Winchester as Camelot, and it was there in the same year that Henry VII's eldest son was baptized as Prince Arthur, to herald the new age. The young prince did not live to be crowned King Arthur and usher in a true new Arthurian age, but his younger brother became Henry VIII and took in the message. He had the Winchester Round Table repainted, with himself depicted at the top as a latter-day Arthur, a Christian emperor and head of a new British empire, with claims once more to European glory, just as Malory and Geoffrey of Monmouth had described.

England was a Catholic medieval state, of course, when Henry had his Round Table painted. A few years later the old world of medieval Christianity in Britain was wiped away in the Protestant Reformation. Glastonbury Abbey was plundered, the tomb of Arthur and Guinevere was smashed and its contents were thrown to the winds. The last abbot was dragged from the abbey on a hurdle and hanged on the Tor. So, even as the Tudors claimed to restore the old British monarchy, they were to sever Britain from its Catholic past, and in a sense from its imaginative past, its cultural roots. With Henry's Reformation the old spirit world was erased, and with it much of the fabric of language, symbols and social ideals that had given birth to the Arthurian legends of the high Middle Ages.

But even if the medieval myth had lost its spiritual basis, it was to enjoy many and varied afterlives in Tudor times, especially as a political fable. The Arthurian myth was revived most famously in Edward Spenser's *The Faerie Queene*, when, in a curious transformation, Elizabeth's mythical descent from the ancient Britons and King Arthur was presented as a Protestant imperial myth, with a pure knighthood obeying the commands of a Virgin Queen and spreading the light of her rule through the world. In the same way her kinsman and successor James I, in uniting the crowns of England and Scotland, would present himself as a new Arthur of Britain. And so, in a curious and roundabout way, the ancient prophecies of Geoffrey of Monmouth had come to pass.

ARTHUR REBORN: THE NINETEENTH-CENTURY REVIVAL

All that, of course, was a fantasy of the ruling class. With revolution, regicide and the Protestant settlement in the seventeenth century, it might be thought that the legend had run its course as a myth central to the needs of political and literary culture in Britain. Indeed, the tale did lose its popularity in the seventeenth century, but great myths that have been built up over hundreds of years don't just disappear. They last because their themes respond to something deep in the minds of their audience, and in the early eighteenth century a funny thing happened.

At the Fountain Coffee House in the Strand in 1720 a group of literary gentlemen founded the Honourable Society of the Knights of the Round Table. In fact, it was claimed at the time that it was a 'refoundation', and that the society really went back to before the battle of Crécy in 1346. Be that as it may, the society is still in existence and still meets on the site of the Fountain, now Simpsons in the Strand. Its goal was the 'perpetuation of the name and fame of King Arthur of Britain and the ideals for which he stood', including 'his Christian endeavour and beliefs'. The society, as it turned out, was the precursor of the nineteenth-century rebirth of Arthur.

As we have already seen in this story, the legend was often re-created in times of crisis and change. At the turn of the nineteenth century, modernity and industrial revolution were on the horizon. There was also a questioning of the past, especially of the old spiritual traditions of Britain and the loss of the pre-Reformation Catholic past. Through the myth, and the rediscovery of the sacred art of the Middle Ages, nineteenth-century people were attempting to renew contact with the world from which they had been irretrievably separated by the Reformation.

The rebirth of Arthur owed a great deal to the rediscovery of Malory's book, which had a tremendous impact when it was republished in several editions in the years after 1800. The perennial vitality of the legend worked its magic again. Its compelling themes struck modern people in the same way that they had thirteenth-century listeners and readers: the quest, the pure knighthood, the fatal union of adulterous love, the deep pathos of civil strife and the ambiguous majesty of kingship itself. All these themes would have a powerful appeal for the Victorians.

Opposite: *The Passing of Arthur,* one of Julia Margaret Cameron's haunting photographs from the 1860s which inspired a host of later treatments and had a big influence on the silent movies.

Thus in the early nineteenth century an Arthurian revival began which was as fervent in its way – and as brilliant – as that in the thirteenth century. When the Houses of Parliament were rebuilt after the disastrous fire of 1834, Arthurian themes from Malory's book were chosen for the decoration of the queen's robing room in the House of Lords, the symbolic centre of the British empire. The plan had the enthusiastic support of Prince Albert himself, although the theme of Guinevere's adultery was thought inappropriate, and the Holy Grail itself was carefully kept out of sight as 'a matter of religious controversy best avoided'. Roman Catholics had only recently been allowed to practise their religion freely, and it was felt that when the queen, the head of the Church of England, was dressing for the highest state occasions, her thoughts were best not distracted by Malory's theological – and very Catholic – interpretation of the grail.

Nevertheless the Victorians were irresistibly drawn to the mystical quasi-religious power of the Arthurian tale. Poems such as Tennyson's *Idylls of the King* and William Morris's *The Defence of Guinevere*, perhaps the greatest Victorian literary treatment of the subject, are testaments to an obsession that runs through their art, poetry and sculpture. It is seen in the fantastically powerful re-creations of the legend by the Pre-Raphaelite painters; and even in the new medium of photography where Julia Margaret Cameron's haunting compositions are a key Victorian visual imagining that has shaped our sensibility and our versions of the tale right down to silent movies and modern Hollywood. Boorman's *Excalibur*, Bresson's *Lancelot* and Sean Connery in *First Knight* are all her children.

The Victorian Arthurian legends were both an expression of pan-British identity – Celtic and Saxon united – and a nostalgic commentary on a lost spirit world. The fragility of goodness, the burden of rule and the impermanence of empire (a deep psychological strain, this, in the whole of nineteenth-century British literary culture) were all resonant themes for the modern British imperialist knights, and gentlemen, on their own road to Camelot. To which one might also add the weird feminization of Arthur in Victoria's empire. Strange as it may seem, as with Elizabeth I the widow of Windsor was in some sense Arthur reborn.

THE MODERN MYTH: A HISTORICAL ARTHUR

And there you might have thought the story of the legend and its many transformations ends. But the Victorian Arthur is not quite the last chapter of the story. For the latest phase of the invention of Arthur is our own. The late twentieth century became one of the greatest of all eras of Arthurian invention. The recent flood of books, films and pictures is a testimony no doubt to the remarkable vitality of the legend, but also to a new twist in the tale: archaeology.

Archaeology arose as a science in the late nineteenth century, when its popular appeal was closely tied to the astonishing discoveries by Heinrich Schliemann in Greece and Turkey, which suggested that behind the myths and legends of Troy there was real history. In our own time British archaeologists set out to find the real Arthur, just as the Glastonbury monks did in 1191. The result was predictably similar. The places chosen for excavation are familiar ones in our tale: Glastonbury, the 'Isle of Avalon'; Cadbury Castle in Somerset, an Iron Age fort which had been claimed as Camelot by Henry VIII's antiquarian John Leland; Tintagel, Arthur's birthplace in Geoffrey of Monmouth's version. In all these places enough clues were found – feasting halls, earthen defences, monastic settlements – to conjure up a convincing Dark Age reality. At Dinas Emrys in Wales excavators even located the pool where, according to Geoffrey of Monmouth, vessels were found containing the two dragons in Merlin's prophecy. Sticking to their sources, nit-picking textual scholars pointed out that none of this proved the existence of Arthur. By now, however, I dare say the idea of the historical Arthur is fixed. Today films, programmes and books about the 'real' Arthur appear every year. In terms of heritage, history and myth, his is the biggest publishing business in Britain. Ironically, then, it is we moderns who have turned the tale into fact. Arthur has finally become real history. How Geoffrey of Monmouth would have laughed!

IRELAND: THE DEEP ROOTS OF STORY

Meanwhile, as twentieth-century archaeology attempted to find a real world of Arthur in the ground, other discoveries were being made that cast the process of the creation of such myths in an entirely different light. Answers were being sought not in archaeological strata, or in documentary texts, but in the nature of story-telling itself. Modern recording of oral tale-tellers in different parts of the world has illuminated the way in which Bronze Age stories like that of Troy came down to bards such as Homer in the Iron Age. They show that behind a written text can lie a story shaped over many centuries by oral transmission. These discoveries have also opened up the deeper currents of Celtic story-telling.

In Ireland many ancient tales in the Gaelic language that were written down in the Middle Ages offer close parallels to the Arthur stories. Finn Macool, for example is, like Arthur, a leader of warriors, one of whom has an affair with Finn's

wife, 'the white enchantress'; Finn's warriors seek a cup; their fellowship dissolves after a last fatal battle – and Finn will also return one day. In Ireland too are stories of magic cauldrons 'which could deliver to any company its suitable food', of a 'victory bringing sword' and a fairy cup that 'revealed all falsehood'. Some of these tales come from a time before the great medieval Arthurian romances, and recently it has become clear that some have been passed down orally for many centuries, if not for thousands of years, and are still circulating in modern Ireland. In the early twentieth century, scholars of Gaelic folklore at University College, Dublin, began to collect these stories from Gaelic-speaking story-tellers, and their extraordinary archive offers an entirely new approach to the genesis of some of the Arthur tales.

Above: Newgrange barrow in the Boyne Valley, Ireland, built by pre-Celtic peoples of the Bronze Age. Perhaps British tale-telling traditions go that far back.

Back in 1983 I went with Seamas O'Cathain to County Mayo in the far west of Ireland to record one of the last of the Gaelic tale-tellers, in the isolated little village of Kilgalligan. John Henry could name the three tale-tellers who had passed the stories down to him, taking the pedigree of his tales back to 1820. He was an old man then, who could neither read nor write, and he did not speak English, but it had taken over ten summers to record his repertoire of tales. When he began to speak it was like a voice from the deep past. His stories of heroes, voyages, battles and adventures were told in forceful, rhythmic prose, full of alliteration and formulas used by oral poets: the roots of his tradition no doubt lay back in the Iron Age. Back in 1983, pursuing Homer, I had been interested in the oral technique itself. Now, thinking about Arthur, I wanted to know more about the Irish hero story. Were story-tellers like John Henry still alive, and what could they tell us about the Arthurian tales?

I retraced my steps to Dublin and to Seamas, who put me in touch with

Professor Daithi O'Hogain. Together Daithi and I listened to tapes of the story-teller Sean O'Duinin made twenty years ago. Then, on a pouring autumn day, we set out from Dublin to find him, driving down past the Rock of Cashel deep into the countryside of County Cork. On the way Daithi told me of the bards, the *fili*, who had been professional transmitters of the hero stories, but who had died out during the devastation of Irish culture by the English in the seventeenth century, when the use of Gaelic had been proscribed. But the old stories had been handed down by tale-tellers among the ordinary people. In a memorizing culture, an oral culture, they were the principal entertainment in the countryside, especially in a land where story-telling was prized above all: 'Ireland will be impoverished,' said one of the bards, 'if there is no telling of tales before bed.'

In a country pub near Kilkenny we met Sean. He is eighty years old now, his fiddle player a sprightly ninety. Gaelic is on the retreat in twenty-first century

Ireland, and Sean is one of only two tale-tellers still alive who can recite the old Gaelic hero tales. He learned them over many years, in the middle of the last century. After him there will be no one to carry on the tradition. A thread thousands of years old will be broken.

In the pub a football match was being shown on a wide-screen TV in the bar while the waitress brought meals to the tables. The fiddle player struck up a jig and ended with a flourish. Then Sean began to speak in a rich rolling Gaelic, which Daithi translated for me. The tale was of the Feanna, the young warriors of the hero Finn Macool. Riding out hunting one day they got lost, and found themselves in an enchanted forest, where there were three weird sisters, the daughters of the Lord of the Forest, who wanted revenge on the Feanna. 'And the daughters have the power of magic, and as soon as the hunters see them they turn three colours and fall rooted to the floor …'

In Sean's tales we could glimpse the deeper images and patterns of Irish story-telling. So it is, too, with the still-living traditions of the *Mahabharata* in India, and the surviving oral stories in Iraq which can be traced back through the tales of the *Arabian Nights* to the mother of all quest stories: the *Epic of Gilgamesh*. Just as there is no end to the world of story, perhaps also there is no beginning …

LAST JOURNEY: THE 'MEN OF THE NORTH'

So there perhaps is a clue to the deep roots of the legend of Arthur. Some of the most famous Arthurian themes and motifs go back long before anything we might call history, let alone anyone we might call Arthur. They are part of the common stock of the tales of Britain; shared Celtic and Irish stories that have their roots in the Iron Age, if not earlier. And yet there are still these nagging questions: Why did legend choose that name? By the same token, why choose Hector, say, or Arjun in the *Mahabharata*? Was there an Arthur after all?

The name appears as Artuir in Irish and north British texts of the sub-Roman period. As it happens, in the *Life of St Columba* written by Adomnan of Iona in around AD 700, there is an undoubted Arthur, unmediated by the fakers, con men

Opposite: Sean O'Duinin (with accordion), one of the last tellers of Gaelic hero stories.
Overleaf: Iona, the sixth-century monastery of St Columba, and burial place of the kings of the Scots. A crossing place between Ireland and northern Britain, it was here that a biography of Columba was written which describes the heroic death in battle of a historical prince Artuir in the late sixth century.

and myth-makers, in an authentic early manuscript. The tale in which he appears takes us full circle: back to the wars of the fifth and sixth centuries described by Gildas … but it is a different tale, and in a different place.

He was Artuir, eldest son of Aedan mac Gabrain, King of Dalriada, the Scottish Dark Age kingdom situated in the Clyde valley. This was a Gaelic-speaking kingdom founded by immigrant tribes from Ireland earlier in the sixth century. Now this Arthur died tragically with one of his brothers in a battle in the 580s or 590s where they defeated an obscure border tribe called the Miathi. The prince's death was remembered, and in Irish annals too because it was the subject of a prophecy by St Columba, which is why the tale is told in his biography.

Artuir fought and died in an area well known to Arthur specialists: the lands between the Firth of Forth and Hadrian's Wall, where we know sub-Roman war-lords continued to hold power long into the Dark Ages. Now this region is also where the earliest Old Welsh poetry comes from: the poems of the bards Aneirin, Taliesin and, interestingly enough, Myrddin, 'the Wild', the wandering fugitive whom Geoffrey of Monmouth turned into Merlin. As we might expect, some of the battles preserved in the bardic tradition go back to this place and time, among them Aneirin's famous poem the *Gododdin*, about the raid on Catterick. The battles remembered by the bards were not all against the Saxons, though; some were against Picts, Scots and Cumbrians. This has been a lawless region fought over throughout history: cattle rustlers, border raiders, war-bands and their leaders have been the subject of songs and stories for centuries. Perhaps this is the kind of context in which a bard in the court of Dalriada might have sung of the victorious but tragic battle prophesied by St Columba, where King Aedan's heir Artuir died fighting with his brothers and 303 heroes of his war-band?

There is one final clue in this north British connection. In the *Annals of Wales*, as we saw earlier, Arthur's last battle took place at a place called Camlann. If this name is represented by any surviving Roman place-name, scholars agree it is the fort of Camboglanna on Hadrian's Wall at Castlesteads, by the river Irthing east of Carlisle. The fort lies south of the Caledonian forest and only a few kilometres from Arthuret, where another famous battle in 573 involved Myrddin, the prototype of Merlin. So why did the tradition name Camlann as Arthur's death place?

Opposite: A view of Hadrian's Wall. The earliest phase of the legend of Arthur perhaps began when poets associated his name with Dark Age battles fought in this region.

THE LAST, DIM, WEIRD BATTLE OF THE WEST

In the forests by Hadrian's Wall is a swift-flowing stream with leaping salmon: a tributary of the Irthing rushes through a winding glen. The steep hillside above is covered with trees, now turning to autumn gold, yellow and brown. The name of the stream is Cam Beck, perhaps preserving the first part of the ancient Roman name. A long, secluded drive leads through the woods to a fine eighteenth-century house, hidden in the forest. Walk on along a muddy path through the woods and soon, under the tangled trees, you make out traces of the embankments of a Roman fort, just visible under thick undergrowth and the remains of an eighteenth-century landscaped garden. In an old potting shed, behind a wooden wheelbarrow and a watering can, is a row of Roman altars and statues, bearing inscriptions to Roman and British gods and goddesses: goddesses of nature and of the forests, Hercules,

Opposite: An inscribed altar to the war god Cocidius from the Roman fort of Camboglanna (Castlesteads).
Above: Cam Beck, the weir below the 'crooked bank' where Hadrian's Wall crosses the Cam Beck. Later Welsh annals suggest this was where Arthur died.

and Cocidius, the Celtic Mars, all cut in the pinkish sandstone from which the fort was built. A civil settlement, probably still inhabited in the sixth century, lies in the fields below. That was when a nearby fort on the Wall at Birdoswald sheltered a spectacular wooden hall, where some unknown British warlord and his warrior band washed their spears and feasted in the sub-Roman twilight.

Walk on through the woods and you come to a steep drop over a sharp curve of Cam Beck: this is the 'crooked bank' (*camboglanna*), which gave the fort its name. From a little wooden footbridge over the stream you can see the weir where Hadrian's Wall crossed the beck. So was this Arthur's Camlann?

The early Welsh poems allow us to imagine the real world of Dark Age British leaders in their feasting halls. They wore golden torcs, or necklaces, and cloaks of beaverskin; they drank 'pale mead' from gilded cups; they fought with 'stained swords and bristling spears', and boasted, so the poets said, that they would 'rather be flesh for wolves than go to the altar to wed'. Leading their mounted war-bands they rode long distances to do battle, like the three hundred heroes killed at Catterick whose praises were later sung in the royal halls of 'the men of the north'; or the Cumbrian host of Urien of Rheged who blockaded the Saxons at Lindisfarne in 575. Was this how it was for another young prince who battled valiantly in the Caledonian forest in the heroic age of Celtic Britain? That, for what it is worth, is my hunch about the 'historical kernel', if such there was. If so, it was small compared with all that followed. Perhaps nothing but the name.

EPILOGUE: THE ONCE AND FUTURE KING

Arthur, I take it then, is essentially a mythical character, like the sleeping hero of Irish legend: one focus of the millennial hopes of the British in the Dark Ages. Stories involving other mythical and historical characters may have become attached to his name in the eighth and ninth centuries, as the English pushed west. By the ninth century Arthur was certainly a figure of legend, although the Arthur we know and love is the literary creation of Norman and post-Norman writers, the collective work of Geoffrey of Monmouth, Chrétien de Troyes and the rest. His story is a body of myths gathered over 1500 years, some of whose themes and motifs go back into the Iron Age, and for all we know maybe even to the pre-Celtic

---

Opposite: *Arthur in Avalon* (1881–98), part of the great canvas by Burne Jones, one of many powerful Victorian reinventions of the tale. The Victorians clearly identified with the weary giant whose noble empire slipped through his fingers.

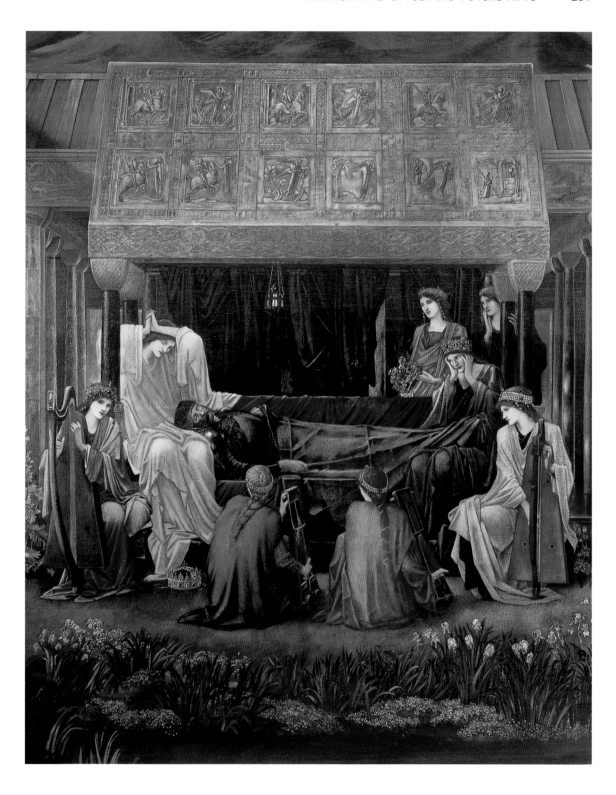

peoples of the Bronze Age. They have probably existed for as long as people have told tales in the islands of Britain.

A last thought, which applies equally to the other myths tracked in these pages. It is about how myths and legends preserve in their tales and their landscapes the 'givenness' of the past despite all the storms of history. The figure of Arthur in the end became a symbol of British history, a living link between the Matter of Britain and the Matter of England. Seen that way, the myth also became a way of exorcizing ghosts and healing the wounds of history – some of which, as we know from conflicts in our own time, can be very long-lasting. In such cases the dry, historical fact offers no solace, prey as it is to the power of the winners. It is myth – Janus-like, protean, shifting – that perhaps offers real consolation, not in literal, historical fact but in poetic, imaginative truth. And a body of myth like the Arthurian tales therefore represents in some magical way the inner life of our history as Britons, over many hundreds, even thousands, of years. Perhaps, therefore, for the people of the British Isles it remains true that, as Thomas Malory said, King Arthur is not dead:

> Yet some men say King Arthur is not dead but had by the will of our Lord Jesus Christ into another place: and men say he shall come again and win the Holy Cross. I will not say it shall be so; but many men say that there is written on his tomb this verse: 'Here lies Arthur: once and future king.'

FURTHER READING

There is no need to overload a book of this kind with a heavy list of references, but here are a few books I have enjoyed reading and found helpful.

THE SEARCH FOR SHANGRI-LA
James Hilton's *Lost Horizon*, first published in 1933, is still in print in the UK from Summersdale Publishers, Chichester. Andrade's account is summarized in C. Wessels, *Early Jesuit Travellers in Central Asia 1603–1721* (1924, reprint 1999). Modern books on the region include Gyurne Dorje's terrific *Tibet Handbook* (1999, new edn forthcoming); S. Batchelor, *The Tibet Guide* (1987 and later edns); and Victor Chan's
Tibet Handbook (1994). For a poignant portrait of Tsaparang in 1949, Lama Govinda, *The Way of the White Clouds* (1960); Govinda's photographs are in Li Gotami Govinda, *Tibet in Pictures* (1979). For a critique of the modern Tibet myth: D. Lopez, *Prisoners of Shangri-La* (1998); see also P. Bishop, *The Myth of Shangri-La* (1989). Charles Allen, *A Mountain in Tibet* (1982) and *The Search for Shangri-La* (1999) and Jon Snelling, *The Sacred Mountain* (1983) are engaging. Edwin Bernbaum gives a very useful summary of the Shambala myth in *The Way to Shambala* (2001), to which I am indebted for details about the sixteenth- and eighteenth-century guidebooks to Shambala. The Dalai Lama is quoted on page 23 from Elaine Brook, *In Search of Shambala* (1996). Tsewang Lama, *Kailash Mandala: a pilgrims' trekking guide* (2002) deserves to be more widely known. On Guge art: P. Pal (ed.), *Himalayas: an Aesthetic Adventure* (2003); the inventory quoted on page 71 is from Roberto Vitali's astonishing re-creation *Records of Tholing: a Literary and Visual Reconstruction of the 'Mother' Monastery in Guge* (1999). The indispensable work on Tibetan religious beliefs is *The Tibetan Book of the Dead*; the first complete translation into English is forthcoming by Gyurme Dorje in Penguin Classics.

JASON AND THE GOLDEN FLEECE
For some versions of the tale: Apollonius is translated in Richard Hunter, *Jason and the Golden Fleece* (1993); for Valerius Flaccus see David Slavitt, *The Voyage of the Argo* (1999); the fifth-century AD Egyptian Orphic version (which some have argued incorporates Iron Age, or even Bronze Age, geography) is in F. Vian, *Les Argonautiques Orphiques* (2002); On Pindar: Charles Segal, *Pindar's Mythmaking: the Fourth Pythian Ode*. On Greek myths in general: a useful compendium, less eccentric than Robert Graves's *Greek Myths*, is T. Gantz, *Early Greek Myth: A Guide to Literary and Artistic Sources*, vol. 1 (1996). On the Medea myth: J. J. Clauss and S. Johnson (eds), *Medea* (1997). The Hittite texts discussed on pages 112–15 are translated in T. Gaster Thespis, *Ritual Myth and Drama in the Ancient Near East* (1961); see on this W. Burkert, *Structure and History in Greek Mythology* (1979); the connections with Jason are argued by V. Haas in *Ugarit-Forschungen 7* (1975). Umberto Eco offers parallels

with the James Bond plots in *Communications 8* (1966). On Greek epic poetry and the Thessaly connection: M. West, 'The Rise of Greek Epic' in *Journal of Hellenic Studies* (1988). For Eastern influence on Greek epic: Walter Burkert, *The Orientalizing Revolution* (1992). On sacrifice and sacredness: Burkert's *Homo Necans* (1983). For a wide-ranging and thought-provoking look at the big story: Marianna Koromila, *The Greeks in the Black Sea* (1991). For a fascinating attempt to sail Jason's route: Tim Severin, *The Jason Voyage* (1984).

THE QUEEN OF SHEBA
On the legend: H. St John Philby, *The Queen of Sheba* (1981) and Marina Warner *From the Beast to the Blonde* (1994); for the Kebra Nagast and the Ethiopian legends see E. Wallis Budge (ed. and trans.), *The Queen of Sheba and Her Only Son Menyelek* (1892). On the archaeology of the Bible: Israel Finkelstein et al., *The Bible Unearthed* (2002). St John Simpson (ed.), *The Queen of Sheba* (2002) is an invaluable catalogue to an exhibition held in the British Museum, with fascinating chapters on the myth and the history. On Axum: a recent very helpful overview is David Phillipson, *Ancient Ethiopia* (1998); see too the same author's *The Monuments of Aksum* (1997), which republishes some of the wonderful photographs from the German excavations of 1906. On Arabia before Islam a recent, very accessible, introduction is Robert G. Hoyland, *Arabia and the Arabs from the Bronze Age to the Coming of Islam* (2001). Among the many travel books about the Incense Coast, one of the most charming is Freya Stark, *The Southern Gates of Arabia* (1936). Of wider relevance to the transformations of the myth, and always stimulating even when infuriating, is Edward Said, *Orientalism* (1991).

ARTHUR: THE ONCE AND FUTURE KING
A vast literature is growing by the year. A still useful introduction to the legends is E. K. Chambers, *Arthur of Britain* (1927). For Geoffrey of Monmouth's *History of the Britons* L. Thorpe (ed) (1966) and later edns; and *The Life of Merlin*, translated by Basil Clarke (1973), with a very helpful introduction. See too S. Echard, *Arthurian Narrative in the Latin Tradition* (1998), and a biography, M. J. Curley, *Geoffrey of Monmouth* (1994). For the latest on the grail: R. Barber, *The Holy Grail* (2004). On the Round Table: Martin Biddle, *King Arthur's Round Table* (2000). On the history: Leslie Alcock, *Arthur's Britain* (2001) is still the best survey of archaeological evidence. [But for a different view see my *In Search of the Dark Ages* (1981) and *In Search of England* (1999).] For an archaeologist's take on the period: Francis Prior, *Britain AD* (2004). On Dark Age links across the Celtic world: E. G. Bowen, *Saints, Seaways and Settlements in the Celtic Lands* (1977). On the Irish background: L. de Paor, *Saint Patrick's World* (1996). Adomnan's *Life of St Columba* is translated by R. Sharpe (1995). For a new take on the parallels in Greek and Eastern legend: Graham Anderson, *King Arthur in Antiquity* (2004). Lastly, for a humane and thought-provoking general work on fairy story and myth: B. Bettelheim, *The Uses of Enchantment* (1991).

ACKNOWLEDGEMENTS

THE SEARCH FOR SHANGRI-LA
In Nepal, my greatest thanks go to Jim and Liz Donovan at the Nepal Trust and
to Tsewang lama, Dan, Jigme and Maya, Rinchen, Kumar and Raju, and all who
made our journey possible. The trust does wonderful work in Nepal and offers
opportunities for outsiders to participate in working holidays on some of its health
projects. Its web site is www. nepaltrust.org. My thanks, too, to the people of the
villages of Jhang, Halji and Til whose great hospitality none of us will ever forget.
In Tibet, Gyurme Dorje was an inspiring guide to the land of Guge; my grateful
thanks to him, and to Tsewang, Tashi and all the Lhasa team who got us to Tsaparang.
In India, I would like to thank Uptal Kumar, Rajiv Chandran and Lakshi
Nishwanathan. In London, Phuntsog Wangyal, and John McGuiness and Miguel
Fialho for providing me with a translation of Andrade.

JASON AND THE GOLDEN FLEECE
My thanks to the island council of Anafe; to the clergy and friends of Zoodochos
Pigi, to Dr Vasiliki Adrimi-Sismani, Marianna Koromila, Maria Powell, Dr Lisa
French, Dr Elias Petropoulos and Dr Pat Easterling. My thanks, too, to Margaret
Kenna, Maria Elena Gorrini and Massimo Cultraro for letting me use their
unpublished research. In Georgia, Valentina Krapchetova-Savvoulidi and the Greek
community of Batumi; Vachtang Chkhvimiani and Richard and their families in
Svaneti; Kevin Tuite and Teimuraz Mamatsashvilit.

THE QUEEN OF SHEBA
My thanks to Dr Bill Glanzman, Gail Warden at the Ethiopian Embassy in London,
Professor Ken Kitchen and Professor Kent Weeks, Lamyah Nasser and all at the
Learning Centre, Quseir, Egypt. St John Simpson and Venetia Porter at the British
Museum, Dr Richard Pankhurst in Addis, Dr David Phillipson, and, in Israel,
Professor Israel Finkelstein and Professor Yair Zakovitch.

ARTHUR: THE ONCE AND FUTURE KING
Thanks to Charles Thomas, Martin Biddle, Ron Hutton, Brian Hinton, Michelle
Brown, Richard Tabor, Seamas O'Cathain, Daithi O'Hogain and the Folklore
department at University College, Dublin, Sean O'Duinin, Rod Lyon, Kathy Jones,
Neil Burridge, Kim Siddhorn and Regia Anglorum, Sue Harris, Richard Neale, Mei
Macintyre-Hugws and Twm Morys, Nancy and Charles Hollingrake, the Johnstone
family at Castlesteads, and Viscount Falkland, Julian Dee and Terence Mallinson.

The films were made by Sean Smith, Jeremy Jeffs, Callum Bulmer, Julian Chatterjee,
Stuart Bruce and Mahmoud Batout: thanks to all for their skill, commitment and
good companionship on the road. Steve Razzetti took the wonderful photos in this
book and I would like to thank him for all his hard work and his always jolly
presence on a demanding series of journeys; thanks also to Madhurima Sen Bose and
all at Earthcare Films, Delhi; Koushik Chatterjee, Ajay Shetty, Sivadas, Darshan
Singh, Nalla and Rajesh; and Sonam Angmo; in Israel, Efrat Suzin and Noam Shaleve

from Highlight Films. In Yemen, Marco Laviotti, Mr Selim and our wonderful drivers the two Abduls. In Egypt, Magdi Rashidy. In Ethiopia, Samson Mckonnen. In Eritrea, Jonah Fisher. In Georgia, Dima Bit-Suleiman. In Greece, Hara Palamidi. In Turkey, Cem Yucesoy.

At Maya Vision Rebecca Dobbs produced the films and as always held everything together with unflagging goodwill; Gerry Branigan was our brilliant and unflappable editor; thanks, also, to Sally Thomas, John Cranmer, Kevin Rowan, Aaron Young and Aleks 'Sacha' Nikolic for all their hard work and good humour in making this project happen. Daisy Newton Dunn did the lion's share of the research; Laura Cooper researched and set up Jason.

At BBC Books thanks to Martin Redfern and Linda Blakemore for their heroic efforts in getting the book together in what was, even for us, record time. I am also very grateful to Sally Potter for her continuing support and encouragement; and to my agent Lavinia Trevor. Thanks, too, to Roly Keating at the BBC for his support; to Krishan Arora; and in the United States to Leo Eaton, John Wilson, Sandy Heberer and all at PBS.

Finally my biggest debt is to my family, to my daughters Jyoti and Mina, and my partner Becky. They put up with my long absences during the making of this series, and I would like to thank them from the bottom of my heart for their love, patience and understanding.

PICTURE CREDITS

INDEX

Page numbers in *italics* refer to illustrations